Blue Laws

Blue Laws

SELECTED & UNCOLLECTED POEMS

1995–2015

KEVIN YOUNG

ALFRED A. KNOPF   NEW YORK   2016

THIS IS A BORZOI BOOK
PUBLISHED BY ALFRED A. KNOPF

Library of Congress Cataloging-in-Publication Data
Young, Kevin.
[Poems. Selections]
Blue laws : selected & uncollected poems, 1995–2015 / Kevin Young.—First edition.
pages ; cm
ISBN 978-0-385-35150-8 (hardcover)—ISBN 978-1-101-94694-7 (eBook)
I. Title.
PS3575.O798A6 2016
811'.54—dc23   2015017451

Front-of-jacket photograph: *My Grandfather's Fiddle* by Kevin Young
Jacket design by Kelly Blair

Manufactured in the United States of America

First Edition

for Keith

Playing the blues in the old days

was like being black twice.

{ LIGHTNING HOPKINS }
as told to Peppermint Harris

CONTENTS

CHAMBER MUSIC [*JELLY ROLL* OUTTAKES, 1999–2004]

HOMAGE TO PHILLIS WHEATLEY [1998–2011]

from DEAR DARKNESS [2008]

BLUE LAWS [*DEAR DARKNESS* OUTTAKES, 2007–2009]

from ARDENCY: A CHRONICLE OF THE *AMISTAD* REBELS [2011]

from BOOK OF HOURS [2014]

PREFACE

Blue Laws gathers poems written over the past two decades, drawing from all nine of my previous published books of poetry and including a number of uncollected, often unpublished, poems. These outtakes range from "Glossolalia," written for an art catalog never realized, to "Rapture," which first appeared in *The New Yorker.* I have generally left these in a rough chronology according to when they were written—or, on rare occasions, placed as part of a separate sequence such as "Homage to Phillis Wheatley"—in order to provide a sense of my process and to gather work of interest that otherwise might go by the wayside. Along the way a very few errors and awkwardnesses have been silently corrected.

In selecting these two-hundred-odd poems I have sought to include pieces regularly read aloud as well as series like "Jack Johnson" or "African Elegy" that help define the books they come from. The main exceptions to this are the book-length poems *To Repel Ghosts*, a "double album" and then remix about the late painter Jean-Michel Basquiat; and the epic *Ardency*, written over twenty years, about the *Amistad* rebellion. I have necessarily limited these selections dramatically. The present volume ends with a selection from the title sequence of *Book of Hours*, a book too recent to select from in great depth, but whose last line comes closest to an epitaph.

The title *Blue Laws* comes from the traditional, often unenforced laws that restrict behavior on the Sabbath, but also speaks to the blues music that informs America's and my own.

—*The Management*

BLUE LAWS

No one to cross a river, but with an authorized ferryman.
No one shall run on the Sabbath day, or walk in his garden or
  elsewhere, except reverently to and from meeting.
No one shall travel, cook victuals, make beds, sweep house,
  cut hair, or shave.
No woman shall kiss her child on the Sabbath or fasting day.

To pick an ear of corn growing in a neighbor's garden, shall
  be deemed theft.
A drunkard shall have a master appointed by the selectmen,
  who are to debar him from the liberty of buying and selling.
Whoever publishes a lie to the prejudice of his neighbor, shall sit
  in the stocks, or be whipped fifteen stripes.
No minister shall keep a school.

Men-stealers shall suffer death.
Whoever wears clothes trimmed with gold, silver, or bone lace,
  above two shillings by the yard, shall be presented by
  the grand jurors, and the selectmen shall tax the offender.
A debtor in prison, swearing he has no estate, shall be let out and
  sold, to make satisfaction.
Whoever brings cards or dice into this dominion shall pay a fine.

No one shall read Common-Prayer, keep Christmas or saint's-days,
  make minced pies, dance, play cards, or play on any instrument
  of music, except the drum, trumpet, and the jaw-harp.
Fornication shall be punished by compelling the marriage,
  or as the Court may think proper.
A wife shall be deemed good evidence against her husband.
Married persons must live together, or be imprisoned.

Every male shall have his hair cut round according to a cap.

from

MOST
WAY
HOME

{ **1995** }

for my family—
blood, adopted, imagined

REWARD

RUN AWAY from this sub-
scriber for the second time
are TWO NEGROES, viz. SMART,
an outlandish dark fellow

with his country marks
on his temples and bearing
the remarkable brand of my
name on his left breast, last

seen wearing an old ragged
negro cloth shirt and breeches
made of fearnought; also DIDO,
a likely young wench of a yellow

cast, born in cherrytime in this
parish, wearing a mixed coloured
coat with a bundle of clothes,
mostly blue, under her one good

arm. Both speak tolerable plain
English and may insist on being
called Cuffee and Khasa respect-
ively. Whoever shall deliver

the said goods to the gaoler
in Baton Rouge, or to the Sugar
House in the parish, shall receive
all reasonable charges plus

a genteel reward besides what
the law allows. In the mean
time all persons are strictly
forbid harbouring them, on pain

of being prosecuted to the utmost
rigour of the law. Ten guineas
will be paid to any one who can
give intelligence of their being

harboured, employed, or enter-
tained by a white person upon
his sentence; five on conviction
of a black. All Masters of vessels

are warned against carrying them
out of state, as they may claim
to be free. If any of the above
Negroes return of their own

accord, they may still be for-
given by

ELIZABETH YOUNG.

HOW TO MAKE RAIN

Start with the sun
piled weeks deep on your back   after
you haven't heard rain for an entire
growing season   and making sure to face
due north   spit twice into the red clay
stomp your silent feet   *waiting rain*
rain to bring the washing in   rain
of reaping   rusty tubs of rain   wish
aloud   to be caught in the throat
of the dry well   head kissing your back
a bent spoon for groundwater   to be
sipped from   *slow courting rain   rain*
that falls forever   rain which keeps
folks inside and makes late afternoon
babies   begin to bury childhood clothes
wrap them around stones   and skulls of
doves   then mark each place well enough
to stand the coming storm   *rain of our*
fathers   shoeless rain   the devil is
beating his wife rain   rain learned
early   in the bones   plant these scare
crow people face down   wing wing
and bony anchor   then wait until they
grow roots and skeletons   *sudden soaking*
rain that draws out the nightcrawler
rain of forgetting   rain that asks for
more rain   rain that can't help but
answer   what you are looking for
must fall   what you are looking for is
deep among clouds   what you want to see
is a girl selling kisses beneath cotton
wood   is a boy drowning inside the earth

VISITING HOME

for Keith

SUNNYMAN:

look there   past
those bitter figs
in the pasture   you can
barely make it out now
but all that you see
all that green   once
was ours

MAMA LUCILLE:

it must have been the summer
before Da Da seemed taller
than everyone   the year your Uncle
Sunnyman was born   the season Keith
stole all your father's well-worn
hard-won   wooden marbles
from a drawer   and shot
them from a slingshot
at the cows   what slow
moving barns
they were

KEITH:

Da Da left out in the heat
his share of mornings   only
to return from the market
in Plaisance with nothing   a hog maybe
sometimes a good sow
but we never had enough
to raise it on   so he slaughtered
what we couldn't keep
gave up the best meat

though he might save
some pigsfeet
for us

MAMA LUCILLE:
when whitemen came with fear
in the night
they told Da Da he had
    to leave
    that was right
    before the war
and land was so tight
people just got crazy

the mosquitoes that June flew big
as horses

we burnt green wood
and the smoke kept them away

KEITH:
the old house stood
about three four mile across the way
you know
where the road runs now
    it was one of those
    old shotgun homes
you could have blasted
right straight through it
in one door and out another

but no one never did

SUNNYMAN:

no one really told me
when it was   they tore
the empty thing down
   Mama had waited a long time
   in that house
   been so many things
mother wife sister queen
guess it wasn't long after Da Da passed on
from that oversized heart
of his   that she weaned me
in this new place   boy, consider yourself
warned: his condition
runs in our family
like you wouldn't believe

MAMA LUCILLE:

it was sunny and my skin ripened
to oranges   I didn't
even have a proper dress
for the funeral
me being pregnant
with Robert and all
so I wore the one with daisies
figured Da Da would like that
just as much   wasn't nearly
as hot that way
but was it ever sunny

KEITH:

there never was a will

Da Da didn't believe in one
he just said the earth
was for whoever needed it most
said we never could own
the land   we just ate
out an ever-emptying hand

some pale man
at the funeral
said the X
by the deed was his
and not Da Da's   and he
could prove it
said we'd have to move
or fight him
and the entire state
of Louisiana

of course we let it go

SUNNYMAN:
folks say this land will never be Young again
that we have lived too long without
so many things that having
seems too hard   but there's one thing
we can never forget: how the land we were
promised is gone   how home for us
is wherever we're not

BEAUTY

before the Sixth Annual
Coushatta Parish
World Fair
& Spectacle

you run
the hotcomb right
through tight,
crowish hair

a smell of lilacs burning
of ripe, half-bitten plums
of waiting by the fire
for the comb to turn colors

once blue
you take the forked iron out
and pull it through until
your roots come straight

or pull out in plugs baked big
as fists, as hands which made
pies from rotting fruit
and ate them while still warm

your hair keeps on
changing to coal
cooling, quiet beneath
your feet

near pig-tailed sisters
who watch and yearn for
the time
they too will burn

in a light this beautiful

from **THE SPECTACLE**

for Colson Whitehead

> *It was a most terrible spectacle. I wish I could commit*
> *to paper the feelings with which I beheld it.*
> —FREDERICK DOUGLASS

THE THIN MAN'S APPRENTICES

Little men born with three heads
of hair, boys of unbroken bones, milk-haters,

boys of lawns & barking roosters, beanpoles
at the sideshow taut holding tents, young men

tying locusts with string, a poor boy's yo-yo.
Father of soft brush, tender-headed boys heading

to barns & avoiding mama's comb, men of prison
haircuts, that bowl around their heads, boys whose ears

outsoar their body, paper airplane kin. Boys of slim
sleep, beds filled with cousins, child of sweet cracklin

& summer spice, boys who ain't hungry, boys living
on love, slipping beneath doors, tightrope

runaways, boys seeing men lynched, boyhood
gone with the circus. Willow men eating soap

to miss the war, seventy-pounds wet, dusky crossing
thresholds, men of harmonica kisses, husbandry,

stomping zydeco night, cigarettes-for-breakfast men,
men of the empty hunt, returning featherless,

hatchet-lunged. Family men, handy men, sturdy
& skinny as rails, hammers waking, John Henry men

racing engines, making do, like love. Men the shade
of bitten apple, red, brown, withering, such wondrous

kite men losing wind, all skin, still soaring, a cross
stretched clear cross the weight of this world.

THE ESCAPE ARTIST

beyond the people
swallowing fire   past the other acts
we had seen before   we found the escape
artist   bound to a chair   hands tied
behind his back   we climbed onstage
to test the chains   around his ankles
and tongue   watched on
as they tucked him   in a burlap sack
and lowered it   into a tank of water
he could get out of   in his sleep

imagine the air   the thin
man   his skin a drum   drawn
across bones   picture disappearing
acts   the vanishing middles
of folks from each town
the man who unsaws them
back together again   dream
each escape   is this easy   that all
you need   is a world full of walls
beardless ladies   and peeling white
fences   that trap the yard   that neighbors
sink their share of ships over   sketch
each side gate   the dirt roads leading
out of town   the dust that holds
no magic   here your feet are locked
to the land   to its unpicked
fields   full of empty
bags of cotton   that no one
ever seems   to work
his way out of

after the hands
on the clock   met seven
times   in prayer   they drew
the artist up   unfolded his cold
body from the sack   and planted
it quietly   on the way out
of town   at home we still hear
his ghost nights   guess he got free
from under the red earth   but what
no one ever asked   is why
would anyone want to

PACHYDERM

just within the circus
of the tattooed man's
skin stood a still bull

elephant brought
and tamed from
the plains of greyest

Africa nails painted red
acrobats with flesh
colored costumes lying

beneath his harmless dark
foot he worked for applause
and peanuts until he grew

used to the weight of clowns
washed white until their feet
seemed tongues

or pendulums on his back
until he grew silent and
toothless a parlor piano

ATLAS

unveiled he stood
before us a living
map to every
thing he thought
he'd seen each side
show or thirsty
mirage tattooed
to his canvas skin
he stole into the colored
half of each town
the Spectacle went
downing white
lightning & nigger
jazz or even stone cold
sober he'd dance
across invisible tracks
to where the gypsies
drew what they
wanted on him covering
the naked stranger
in sphinxes & pearly
devils for his silver

he began to love
the babylon they
were building he
felt at home filling
his arms & stomach
with their story or
holding the negresses
until dawn showing
them the painted heaven
of his arms the pictures
of dead africans winging
their way home or
seizing the wrists
of whores their *O my*
lords among feathers
& dragonflies

still he never went
past the bounds
of good taste no
design ever slipped
past wrist or adam's
apple no quadroon
ever took his arm
in public with a shirt
on he was quite
respectable it was
only pants off that
they couldn't stop
kissing the thin
underworld of his
legs one buried in
thick jaundice
flame the other
draped in burning
snow that bluish
shade of winter
rarely seen
this far south

but as we circled
around that day
the sun beating
down on the seas
of his shoulders
no one offered
him a mirror no
body showed him
the pale horizon
of his spine or
the boundless
blue of his back
none of us pointed
out the ships full
of people their future
stowed with small seeds
of okra among thick
rooted hair

with his back
to us we wanted
more than any
thing to reach
into the very small
of his spine stirring
the shallows reaching
down among stones
& voiceless shells
diving past that white
hot core to the other
side to where folks
walked on their hands
hoping to find that
continent drowned
beneath calm sight
less skin

later in our kitchen
we told grandma
about the man who
was drawn she stopped
shelling peas & called
us to her undoing
the unmatched buttons
of her shirt she said
when I was carrying
my first & tried
to run the horse
men caught me dug
me a hole for my
child & laid me
belly down in it then
gathered round
like the Spectacle
they whipped me
inside out slowly she
took off her blouse
baring her back
that long ladder
of scars climbing into
her hair *listen* she
continued *what he*
believes he been holding
all these years that aint
a world at all: it's me

REVIVAL

came early with
June, each tent a hot
angel of healing, the Spirit
catching in women's throats
and anointing the lazy eye
of an uncle. You wanted
nothing more than for that
preacherman from way
out west to lay golden
hands upon you, making
your pain that thing
he spoke of

until you became
a testimony circling
the tent on your own. Lord
how you prayed that week
your knees turning into
the hard-backed pews of early
service, each with a brassy
name in its side; how you
went back each

and every night
filling the aisles with
bodies better left
behind. Back then sin
was a coin rubbed
faceless in the pocket
an offering given
gladly, that clear silver
sound everyone
listened for.

from **SAYING GRACE**

for my mother

THE LIVING

I.

After Independence Day
all our toys began to tear
up, school growing sweet

on our tongues. We had
already cut & hoed
the cotton into rows, weeds

piled useless as Confederate
bills. September meant picking
& half-days at Springfield, us colored

grades let off at noon to pick
the valuable white till
nightfall. My hands, civil

& slow, didn't even deserve
my behind on the picking truck,
but Unc Chock ran the thing

& Mama would've killed him dead
if he'd dreamt of trying
to get salty. The money was bad

like all money then, not near
as green or wide. Three dollars
for a hundred pounds, better part

of a day. I barely kept up, hands swole up
like unpicked fruit. No matter when
she started, Frankie plucked fifteen pounds

more, food for two, a new
Easter dress. Summers I turned
so black & bent, all because I'd rather

pick with friends than sling weeds
alone, than stuff my mattress green.

   2.
Winters, when the white king
had gone, we slept like fish, still
moving. We walked back home
for lunch & retraced after school, changing
into our other pair of drawers
before we chored the stove's ash. No one

got gas till after the War. Each November
brought a boxcar from the Atchison
Topeka & Santa Fe; for a share,
Lopez balanced it home on his flatbed,
a whale from the hunt. Once full
of hobos, that belly we burnt kept us

from freezing all season long. Before
tossing each board in, I would run
my hands across the wood speech
of bums, carvings warning
Unfriendly Conductor, Town of No
Sleep. Leftover wood turned

to toys; three boards & somebody's
old rollerskate became a summer
scooter. Bored, what was that?
We were too busy being poor
in that house air-conditioned all winter,
too busy sharing everything, even

bathwater evenings by the pipe stove.
No plumbing, no rats, only mice thick
enough to believe we had more
than they did.

THE SLAUGHTER

I.

Everything we ate was on foot. We didn't have
the Norge or the Frigidaire, only salt to keep.
Autumn's hog went in brine for days,
swimming. You had to boil forever
just to get the taste out. I loved winter
& its chitlins, but boy I hated cleaning.
If not from the hogs, we got fresh bucketsful
from our slaughterhouse kin. White folks
got first pick, even of guts. They loved

that stuff, but to us it was only a season, just
making do. Home, you cut innards in strips,
put water in one end, held the other tight
then seesawed them back & forth. Afterwards
we dumped the excess in a hole dug out
back. I always make sure folks clean them
a second time. Don't eat chitlins
at just anyone's filthy old house.

2.

Chickens went like dusk. Before
twilight, Mama said go get me a hen
& me in that swept yard, swinging one round
by the neck, the pop, then dropping it.
We wrung, but some folks chopped, the chicken
flapping awhile before it fell, headless, a sight.
Feathers we plucked told us that soon
cold would come indoors like greens after

first frost. Everything then tasted so different
& fresh, a sister's backtalk, but I wouldn't want
back those days for all the known world.
No sir. Some nights dinner would just get up
& run off cause I hadn't wrung it right,
others we'd eat roosters tougher
& older than we were, meat so rough Mama
couldn't cut it with her brown, brown eyes.

THE KITCHEN

Heard tell Mama's
white folks were fair
cause they didn't turn her
to bone—only later
did I understand good

wasn't just Unc Chock's hair
but meant the father
didn't want to make her,
meant they paid her decent
so's Mama didn't need

to smuggle home silver,
knife tucked between cuff
& wrist. Still drove me
crazy the way no one
saw clear to pick her up—

then again she probably
would have refused, saying
she liked the walk, more likely
not wanting their family
to know our business. Even now

the son calls her Aunt
as if she never had a whole
nother house full
of mouths. After she'd dusted
& cooked & the dog'd been fed

she fixed herself a little
something, wrapping us
a plate of what whites
called leftovers, but we
knew as leavings:

fugitives of fat dark
meat the mother didn't like;
brown bags of broken cookies
we weren't allowed
to eat till we cleaned

our plates. No matter
how nice Mama's whites were,
the father made her enter
the back way like a cat
burglar, black dress & all—

she'd stay in the kitchen,
the same place her naps hid
between visits to the salon,
back of her head where the heat
couldn't reach, where we knew

she stowed a second set of eyes.

THE QUENCH

Thirst kept with us all
year. Yellow
hands rolled till soft
enough for lemonade, pulp
mixed with sugar
to stop us from wincing.

Water then was clean
as Fifth Sunday sermon.

We weren't the Nehi family
that Frankie's was, heavy
bottles of Coke & orange
nosing against each other
in her icebox, glass pressed
like noses at toyshop
windows. Such swallowed
luxury, small as it was, never got

opened for guests. Guess
that made me kin, her cola brown

flowing in my blood too. Cherry,
grape, my house swam mostly
in Kool-Aid, red staining
our mouths like play
draculas often enough
I don't much
care for it now.

Nickel a packet, six
for a quarter, each flavor

made two honest quarts. Enough
to fill us children with silence
long after the wake, well
past the summer Frankie fell
down the well & stayed
there, soaking up that clear,
careless sky.

THE PRESERVING

Summer meant peeling: peaches,
pears, July, all carved up. August
was a tomato dropped
in boiling water, my skin coming
right off. And peas, Lord,
after shelling all summer, if I never
saw those green fingers again
it would be too soon. We'd also
make wine, gather up those peach
scraps, put them in jars & let them
turn. Trick was enough air.

Eating something boiled each meal,
my hair in coils by June first, Mama
could barely reel me in from the red
clay long enough to wrap my hair
with string. So tight
I couldn't think. But that was far
easier to take care of, lasted all
summer like ashy knees.
One Thanksgiving, while saying grace
we heard what sounded like a gunshot
ran to the back porch to see
peach glass everywhere. Reckon
someone didn't give the jar enough

room to breathe. Only good thing
bout them saving days was knowing
they'd be over, that by Christmas
afternoons turned to cakes: coconut
yesterday, fruitcake today, fresh
cushaw pie to start tomorrow.
On Jesus' Day we'd go house
to house tasting each family's peach
brandy. You know you could stand
only so much, a taste. Time we weaved
back, it had grown cold as war.
Huddling home, clutching each
other in our handed down hand-
me-downs, we felt we was dying
like a late fire; we prayed
those homemade spirits
would warm most way home.

WHATEVER YOU WANT

for Arnold Kemp

This could be a good day. It starts
without you, as usual; you haven't seen
dawn in years. By noon it hits half-
boiling & the air breaks down. After lunch
even the fans turn lazy, not moving you
or wind. Is it the Negro in you that gets
in the car & just starts driving, keeps
the windows down, your music
bouncing off station wagons, power
windows? Whatever you want

to call it, it makes you feel you own
everything, even the creeping heat. Spin
the radio looking for summer, for love
songs with someone somewhere worse
off than you. Why doesn't anyone
advertise for rain? Instead the personalities
keep talking to prove they are indoors,
cool. By seven the temperature outsails
the price of gas, the movies are all sold out
& you can't get cool for the heavens.

So peel away, head for the edge
of town where the roads turn thin & alone,
speeding to prove you can summon death
like tortoises cracked open in the road
up ahead, the water stored in their shells
running free. Keep on trying to out-race
heat's red siren until radio sings out

Come home, come on home black boy
to your chimney full of birds, to this house
of flame. Evening, the heat holds you
with its aching, unavoidable fingers;
you sleep naked, dreamless to heat.
Windows thrown open as mouths, fan on,
it still feels like a ghost is baking sweet
potato pies through the night. Your favorite.

CLYDE PEELING'S REPTILAND
IN ALLENWOOD, PENNSYLVANIA

You must admit it's natural
that while waiting for the three o'clock
informational reptile handling & petting

show, we all imagined a few choice tragedies,
maybe a snake devouring one of the six
identical blond children in the front row,

or the anaconda choking on all five
badly braided girls. I confess openly
we discussed ways in which the obnoxious

crying child in the third row actually wriggled
free of daddy's constricting arms, his head opened
against the ground like a melon & a ripe one

at that. See, in the end the tragedy is all
in the telling, not at the moment when the gator
slips out of Ched Peeling's trusty, thoroughbred

hands & gobbles down a few select
youngsters—preferably the really loud or
beautiful ones—but later, after the ambulances

have sped away & no one breathes
a word. Even when everything is said
& done, I don't know whether only the loud

& really beautiful things get remembered
or most things just grow loud & beautiful
when gone. I can only tell you

that later I thought for hours about Irvy
the Alligator's smooth underbelly & the way
it drove him nearly extinct, how folks once

looked at him & called him desire, a handbag
in waiting. How you won't drive past any Negrolands
on your way through Pennsylvania, or anywhere

else in this union. How while learning about lizards
that grow their tails back, bloodless, I kept
thinking The Colored Zoo may be exactly what

we need, a pleasant place to find out how They eat
watermelon & mate regularly, a cool comfortable
room where everyone can sit around

& ask *How do I recognize
one or protect myself?* or *Their hair,
how do They get it to clench up*

like that? A guide dressed in unthreatening
greens or a color we don't have to call
brown could reply *Good question,*

then hold one up & demonstrate, show
all the key markings. But you must
believe me when I say there is not really

such a place, when I tell you that I held
my breath with the rest at Reptiland, listening
to Ched recite his snakebite story for the four-

hundredth time, waving around his middle finger
where the rattler sunk fangs. You must forgive
how we leaned closer as he described venom

eating green & cold through his veins, pictured
perfectly its slow nauseous seep, like watching
the eleven o'clock footage of someone beaten

blue by the cops, over & over, knowing you could
do nothing about this, only watch, knowing
it already has all happened without you

& probably will keep on happening, steady
as snake poison traveling toward the heart,
the way these things go on by, slowly,

an ancient turtle we pay
to pet as it walks past,
souvenir, survivor.

EVERYWHERE IS OUT OF TOWN

for Maceo Parker & the JB Horns

Beanville. Tea
party. Five black cats
& a white boy. Chitlin
circuit. Gravy colored suits,
preacher stripes. Didn't
know you could buy
muttonchops these days.
Afros. Horns slung
round necks like giant
ladles. Dressing. Uptempo
blessing: *Good God*

everywhere! We bow our
heads before the band
lets loose. Drummer unknown
as a hymn's third verse.
Older woman pushes toward
the front, catching the spirit
like the crazy lady at church
six scotches later. Communion

breath. Hands waving. Sweaty
face rags, post-sermon
mop, suicidal white girls crying
like the newly baptized. All that
water. Play it. Swing
it. *Be suggestive.* Request
"Chicken" & "Pass the Peas"
like we used to say. Have mercy!
Thanksgiving's back in town

& we're all crammed in the club white
as the walls of a church basement. Feet
impatient as forks. Only ten bucks
a plate for this leftover band. Thigh,
drumsticks, neck. Dark meat.

EDDIE PRIEST'S
BARBERSHOP & NOTARY

Closed Mondays

is music   is men
off early from work   is waiting
for the chance at the chair
while the eagle claws holes
in your pockets   keeping
time   by the turning
of rusty fans   steel flowers with
cold breezes   is having nothing
better to do   than guess at the years
of hair   matted beneath the soiled caps
of drunks   the pain of running
a fisted comb through stubborn
knots   is the dark dirty low
down blues   the tender heads
of sons fresh from cornrows   all
wonder at losing   half their height
is a mother gathering hair   for good
luck   for a soft wig   is the round
difficulty of ears   the peach
faced boys asking Eddie
to cut in parts and arrows
wanting to have their names read
for just a few days   and among thin
jazz   is the quick brush of a done
head   the black flood around
your feet   grandfathers
stopping their games of ivory
dominoes   just before they reach the bone
yard   is winking widowers announcing
cut it clean off   I'm through courting
and hair only gets in the way   is the final
spin of the chair   a reflection of
a reflection   that sting of wintergreen

tonic   on the neck of a sleeping snow
haired man   when you realize it is
your turn   you are next

QUIVIRA CITY LIMITS

for Thomas Fox Averill

Pull over. Your car with its slow
breathing. Somewhere outside Topeka

it suddenly all matters again,
those tractors blooming rust

in the fields only need a good coat
of paint. Red. You had to see

for yourself, didn't you; see that the world
never turned small, transportation

just got better; to learn
we can't say a town or a baseball

team without breathing in
a dead Indian. To discover why Coronado

pushed up here, following the guide
who said he knew fields of gold,

north, who led them past these plains,
past buffaloes dark as he was. Look.

Nothing but the wheat, waving them
sick, a sea. While they strangle

him blue as the sky above you
The Moor must also wonder

when will all this ever be enough?
this wide open they call discovery,

disappointment, this place my
thousand bones carry, now call home.

LETTERS FROM THE NORTH STAR

Dear you: the lights here ask
nothing, the white falling
around my letters silent,
unstoppable. I am writing this
from the empty stomach of sleep

where nothing but the cold
wonders where you're headed;
nobody here peels heads sour
and cheap as lemon, and only
the car sings AM the whole

night through. In the city,
I have seen children half-
bitten by wind. Even trains
arrive without a soul
to greet them; things do

not need me here, this world
dances on its own. Only bridges
beg for me to make them
famous, to learn what I had
almost forgotten of flying,

of soaring free, south,
down. So long. Xs, Os.

GLOSSOLALIA

{ 1997 }

GLOSSOLALIA

DARK EY:

Shoeless dust. Trusting, yassuh,
a rusty musk. Blank. Thank
you, no. Lil' Bo Peep done
lost her sheep. And shall not want—

DINGE:

Wormwood. Silent wall too tall
to scale. To set afire to, the cork
burnt then smeared till
it darkens the skin. Dancin'. Pork.

O FAY:

An openness. She say: it come
not from foe, not from pig
latin. It mean a wooden thing
a doll. Desire. Totem or toll.

GRAY:

They know not. No.
They. What an invisible
man saw, his shadow—
ours. Ain't no thang—

NIGRA:

A needle, the shallow
well which the gal
got lost in. Called out
your name. Boy, sit up straight.

BUCK:

Hooded. The veil. The tail
wagging. The dog. Bull-
frog full-lipped. Kiss
me & I turn. It's on you—

CRACK ER:
Fish oil & salt water wafer.
A whip. The sting—
words which weight. Cheap
skate. Ritz. Laundry lists.

RED NECK:
Honest Injun. Big gyp.
Bust lip. Bum
leg. Frog catching. Throats.
Lawn boats. Boasts—

NE GRESS:
Stunt double. Laundry
lists. Complaints. Ain'ts.
Sardines. Shipped spoon-
style. Mock smile.

GLOS´ ə LA´ LE

1. Fabricated and nonmeaningful
speech, esp. such speech associated
with certain schizophrenic syndromes.
2. The gift of tongues.

1997

44

from

TO REPEL GHOSTS

●

— **SUNG BY THE AUTHOR** —

{ **2001**; **remix 2005** }

NEGATIVE

Wake to find everything black
what was white, all the vice
versa—white maids on TV, black

sitcoms that star white dwarfs
cute as pearl buttons. Black Presidents,
Black Houses. White horse

candidates. All bleach burns
clothes black. Drive roads
white as you are, white songs

on the radio stolen by black bands
like secret pancake recipes, white back-up
singers, ball-players & boxers all

white as tar. Feathers on chickens
dark as everything, boiling in the pot
that called the kettle honky. Even

whites of the eye turn dark, pupils
clear & changing as a cat's.
Is this what we've wanted

& waited for? to see snow
covering everything black
as Christmas, dark pages written

white upon? All our eclipses bright,
dark stars shooting across pale
sky, glowing like ash in fire, shower

every skin. Only money keeps
green, still grows & burns like grass
under dark daylight.

CAMPBELL'S BLACK BEAN SOUP

Candid, Warhol
scoffed, coined it
a nigger's loft—

not The Factory,
Basquiat's studio stood
anything but lofty—

skid rows of canvases,
paint peeling like bananas,
scabs. Bartering work

for horse, Basquiat churned
out butter, signing each
SAMO©. Sameold. Sambo's

soup. How to sell out
something bankrupt
already? How to copy

rights? Basquiat stripped
labels, opened & ate
alphabets, chicken

& noodle. Not even brown
broth left beneath, not one
black bean, he smacked

the very bottom, scraping
the uncanny, making
a tin thing sing.

POISON OASIS { 1981 }

Such church hurts—
all haloes, crowns,
coins ancient,

flattened. Cross-
roads. Money changes
hands stained

like glass. Mirror,
mirage—the dog
a praying mantis at his

feet. Basquiat eyes
the needle, needs
a fix—if the camel fits—

heaven. *Gimme*
some smack
or I'll smack

you back. Which side
should he pierce,
where to place

the dromedary
in his vein? Each opening
fills with wine

a wound. Hollowed
ground. Blood
of our blood—

Basquiat trades
Golgotha, skulls
& all, for an armful

of stigmata.
Runs a game,
plays snakes

& ladders, shooting
up. SAMO says: IF SOMEONE
SMITES YOU, TURN

THE OTHER FACE.
Even falling
has its grace—injection

& genuflection
both bring you
to your knees,

make you prey.

CADILLAC MOON { 1981 }

Crashing
again—Basquiat
sends fenders

& letters headlong
into each other,
the future. Fusion.

A A A A A A A A A A.

Big Bang. The Big
Apple, Atom's,
behind him—

no sirens
in sight. His career
of careening

since—at six—
playing stickball
a car stole

his spleen. Blind
sided. Move
along folks—nothing

to see here. Driven,
does two Caddys
colliding, biting

the dust he's begun
to snort. Hit
& run. Red

Cross—the pill-pale
ambulance, inside
out, he hitched

to the hospital.
Joy ride. Hot
wired. O the rush

before the wreck—

each Cadillac
a Titanic,
an iceberg that's met

its match—cabin
flooded
like an engine,

drawing even
dark Shine
from below deck.

FLATS FIX. Chop

shop. Body work
while-u-wait. *In situ*
the spleen

or lien, anterior view—
removed. Given
Gray's Anatomy

by his mother for recovery—

151. Reflexion of spleen
turned forwards
& to the right, like

pages of a book—
Basquiat pulled
into orbit

with tide, the moon
gold as a tooth,
a hubcap gleaming,

gleaned—Shine
swimming for land,
somewhere solid

to spin his own obit.

BROTHERS SAUSAGE { 1983 }

The trees told nobody
what, that day, we did—
we died. Laid down

with our cans
of deviled
ham & closed

our eyes—two
valises full
of Van Camp's

Pork & Beans—
the city an idea
shining far behind—

& we were not afraid

just terrified
of bears, of basic
black—the night—

white hunters
with their plaid
& pop-guns—

sleep was our bag—
a body—we began
to crave our beds

even empty & unmade
as a mind—
the silence & sounds

of nature scared us—

WORLD WORLD
FAMOUS—
EST 1897

COTTON,
SLAVES, IN MAY A
DERANGED—

this Indian
land given
no heed, taken

back & turned to park—

BEEF PORK SALT
WATER CORN
SYRUP SOLIDS

guns loaded
like a question,
aimed—imagine—

shhhh—be vewy
vewy quiet, we're
hunting wabbits—

DARWIN.
ALLAH. BUDDHA.
BLUE RIBBON.

MALCOLM X
VS. AL JOLSON—
whistling Dixie,

we pack up
like meat—ACME—
to the city—

RINSO

Grace—that's Miss
Jones to you—
done up

like the devil, old
Kali. Collared,
leopard

skinned—crouched
in a cage
her white photographer

& husband, placed
her in. Big
game. THE MOST

AMAZING DEVELOPMENT
IN SOAP
HISTORY. Butcher,

Maker, Josephine Baker
walked her leopards,
leashed, down

the Champs-Elysées
head high. KINGFISH.
SAPPHIRE. *I'm not*

perfect
but I'm perfect
for you—keeping

up, Jones goes
wild like a card.
Spade. THEM

SHOVELS. Joker,
queen, deuce
deuce—face

painted blue
by Warhol, her body
done in

white by Haring—
same as Bill T
Jones (no reln)

his cock striped
white, skunked.
Vein.

What a doll—
she wants to wear
Haring's radiant

babies, pale crosses,
tribal headdress
& all, to the ball. Little

else. Cinder-
ella has nothing
on Grace—

NO SUH
NO SUH
princess

& step-
sister rolled
into one. IL FOOL.

SLOGAN.
If the soft
shoe fits . . .

Diva, devil
may care—
she's riding high

as fashion. *Love*
is the drug
& she's here

to score.
Slave

to the rhythm, rinse
—repeat—WHITE
WSHING ACTION—

JACK JOHNSON

1982, acrylic & oil paintstick on canvas

Jack decided that being a painter was less of a vocation than he had supposed. He would be a boxer instead. He had the punch; he had the speed; he was capable of moving half a second before trouble arrived in his neck of the woods.

{ DENZIL BATCHELOR }

Jack Johnson & His Times

BLACK JACK { B. 31 MARCH 1878 }

Some call me spade,
stud, buck, black. That last
I take as compliment—

"I am black & they
won't let me forget it."
I'm Jack

to my friends, Lil'
Arthur—like that King
of England—to my mama.

Since I got crowned champ
most white folks would love
to see me whupped.

They call me dog, cad
or card, then bet
on me to win. I'm still

an ace & the whole
world knows it. Don't
mean most don't want

me done in. But I got words
for them too—when I'm through
most chumps wish

they were counting
cash instead
of sheep, stars. I deal

blows like cards—
one round, twenty
rounds, more. "I'm black all

right & I'll never let them
forget it." Stepping
to me, in or out

the ring, you gamble—
go head then dealer,
hit me again.

And there had come into prominence a huge negro, Jack
Johnson, who was anxious to fight Burns. In England we
had hitherto heard very little of Johnson. He was three
years older than the white champion, stood 6 feet and one-
half inch, and weighed 15 stone. He appears to have started
his career in 1899, and from that year down to December,
1908, when he finally succeeded in getting a match with
Burns, he had fought sixty-five contests, half of which he
won by means of a knockout. . . . He was very strong, very
quick, a hard hitter, and extraordinarily skilful in defence.
He was by no means unintelligent, and not without good
reason, was regarded generally with the greatest possible
dislike. With money in his pocket and physical triumph
over white men in his heart, he displayed all the gross and
overbearing insolence which makes what we call the buck
nigger insufferable.

—BOHUN LYNCH
Knuckles & Gloves, 1923

THE UPSET { 26 DECEMBER 1908 }

"Who told
you I was yellow?"
I wanted to know

taunted—"Come
& get it
Lil Tahmy"

in my best English
accent, inviting
Burns to dodge

my fists the way
he'd avoided me,
running

farther—Britain
France—than
that kangaroo

I once bet I could
outdistance & did.
Chased down

to Sydney
Stadium, now was nowhere
to go—no more

color line to hide
behind, no lies bout
my coward streak—

I will bet a few plunks
the colored man
will not make good!

That I wasn't game.
Baited him
like a race—first

round he fell
with his odds,
favored. By two

all bets were even
& I made him pay—drew
blood—pounded

his face into morse, worse
than what Old Teddy
Roosevelt could stand

to hear over the wire. Bully.
"You're white, dead
scared white

as the flag of surrender.
You like to eat
leather?" By twelve I bet

he wished
he was still
at sea, had stayed Noah

Brusso, not Burns
trapped in Rushcutters Bay
about to be smoked

like my finest
cigar. "Didn't
they tell us this

boy was an in-
fighter?"
By thirteen

rounds he bites
luck & dust—
the police

rush in like fools,
angels, afraid
for both of us

treading this ring
like water,
my wide wake.

There is no use minimizing Johnson's victory in order
to soothe Burn's feelings. It is part of the game to take
punishment in the ring, and it is just as much part of the
game to take unbiased criticism afterwards in the columns
of the Press. Personally I was with Burns all the way. He
is a white man, and so am I. Naturally I wanted to see the
white man win.

—JACK LONDON
Jack London Reports

THE CROWN { 4 JULY 1910 }

In order to take
away my title
Jeffries—Great White

Hope—emerged
like a whale, lost
weight, spouted

steam. Said Negroes
have a soft spot
in our bellies

that only needs
finding. Bull's
eye. He refused

our pre-fight shake—
my eyes clear
like the time, years

later, I saw Rasputin
at the Czar's Palace
weeks before the Reds

stormed in, & knew that big
man—whom no one could
outdrink or talk—was grand

but finished. Heard
it took five tries
—poison, stabbing, more—

before he went at last
under. Jeffries was cash
by round one. Fresh

from his alfalfa
farm retirement,
only he was fool

or good enough
to challenge me, stage
a bit of revolution—

the Whites
couldn't have
me running

their show, much less
own the crown.
Called for my head.

"Devoutly hope
I didn't happen
to hurt you, Jeff"—

my fists harpoons,
hammers of John
Henry gainst

that gray engine
—*I think I can*—
steaming. Stood

whenever in my corner
facing the sun
after giving him

the shady one.
My trunks navy
blue as Reno

sky, Old Glory
lashed through
the loops—that Independence

Day, despite warning
shots & death threats
before the match,

I lit Jeffries like black
powder, a fire
cracker—

on a breakfast
of 4 lamb cutlets,
3 eggs, some steak

beat him till he
hugged me
those last rounds

& I put him
out his misery.
You could hear the riots

already—from Fort
Worth & Norfolk,
Roanoke to New

York, mobs
gather, turning
Main Street into a main

event, pummeling
any black cat
who crosses

their paths.
Neck tie
parties—cutting

another grin
below any raised
Negro chins—

JOHNSON WINS
WHITES LYNCH
70 ARRESTED

BALTIMORE
OMAHA NEGRO
KILLED—

all because I kept
their hope
on the ropes. His face

like newsprint
bruised. On account
of my coal-fed heart—

caboose red
& bright
as his—what wouldn't give.

Amaze an' Grace, how sweet it sounds,
Jack Johnson knocked Jim Jeffries down.
Jim Jeffries jumped up an' hit Jack on the chin.
An' then Jack knocked him down agin.

The Yankees hold the play,
The white man pull the trigger;
But it makes no difference what the white man say,
The world champion's still a nigger.

—TRADITIONAL

THE RING { 13 MAY 1913 }

The bed is just
another ring I'd beat
them white boys in—

double, four
poster, queen.
I'd go the rounds

with girls who begged
to rub my head
cause it was clean

shaven, polished.
Said it felt like billiards
to them, bald

black. Balling
was fine, but once
I began to knock out

their men & sweep
the women off their feet
—even bought one a ring—

well, that was too much.
When I exchanged vows
with my second wife

—before God & everyone—
they swore I'd pay. Few
could touch me anyway,

what did I care. Later
when she did herself in
in our bed, I knew

—sure as standing—
they'd pushed her
to the edge. After

I mourned & met
my next love
& wife—my mama,

Tiny, said
little but worry—
they trumped

up charges, 11 counts
of the Mann Act
so I couldn't fight. My dice

role came up thirteen—
a baker's dozen
of prostitution & white

slavery—a white jury
after one hour found me
guilty of crimes

versus nature. Put
me through the ringer.
Nigras, you see, ain't

supposed to have brains
or bodies, our heads just
a bag to punch. But I beat

the rap without fists—
disguised as a Black
Giant, I swapped

gloves—boxing
for baseball—traded
prison stripes for Rube

Foster's wool
uniform. Smuggled
north into Canada

like chattel, we sailed
the *Corinthian*
for England, staying below

deck. Fair France
greeted me with a force
of police—turns out to tame

the cheering crowds—
granted me amnesty,
let me keep my hide

whether world
champ, con, or stripped
like my crown.

Jack Johnson's case will be settled in due time in the courts.
Until the court has spoken, I do not care to either defend or
condemn him. I can only say at this time, that this is another
illustration of the most irreparable injury that a wrong
action on the part of a single individual may do to a whole
race. It shows the folly of those who think that they alone
will be held responsible for the evil that they do. Especially
is this true in the case of the Negro in the United States
today. No one can do so much injury to the Negro race as the
Negro himself. This will seem to many persons unjust, but
no one can doubt that it is true.

What makes the situation seem a little worse in this
case, is the fact that it was the white man, not the black
man who has given Jack Johnson the kind of prominence
he has enjoyed up to now and put him, in other words, in a
position where he has been able to bring humiliation upon
the whole race of which he is a member.

—BOOKER T. WASHINGTON
for United Press Association
23 October 1912

Some pretend to object to Mr. Johnson's character. But we have yet to hear, in the case of white America, that marital troubles have disqualified prizefighters or ball players or even statesmen. It comes down then, after all, to this unforgiveable blackness. Wherefore we conclude that at present prizefighting is very, very immoral, and that we must rely on football and war for pastimes until Mr. Johnson retires or permits himself to be "knocked out."

—W. E. B. DU BOIS
Crisis, August 1914

THE FIX { 5 APRIL 1915 }

That fight with Willard was a fix
not a faceoff. Out of the ring
three years, jonesing

for the States, I struck a deal
to beat the Mann
Act—one taste of mat

& I'd get
let back home.
But I even told

my mama—
Tiny,
Bet on me.

Once in the bout—run out
of Mexico by Pancho
Villa himself—I fought that fix

the way, years back, Ketchel
knocked me down
even after we'd shook

& agreed I'd take the fall
if he carried me
the rounds without trying

to KO—crossed,
doubled
over, I stood up & broke

his teeth like
a promise. At the root.
On the canvas

they shined, white
as a lie. But with Willard
that spring, each punch

was a sucker, every round
a gun. Loaded. Still
I fixed him—strung

him along the ropes
for twenty-five
rounds. At twenty-six

the alphabet in my head
gave way—saw
my wife take the take,

count our fifty grand
& leave. Did the dive,
shielding my eyes—

not so much from Havana
heat—its reek my favorite
cigar—as from the ref's count.

Down, I counted too, blessings
instead of bets. Stretched
there on the canvas

—a masterpiece—stripped
of my title, primed
to return to the States.

Saved. Best
believe I stood up
smiling.

If you tonight suddenly should become full-fledged
Americans; if your color faded, or the color line here in
Chicago was miraculously forgotten: suppose, too, you
became at the same time rich and powerful;—what is it
that you would want? What would you immediately seek?
Would you buy the most powerful of motor cars and outrace
Cook County? Would you buy the most elaborate estate
on the North Shore? Would you be a Rotarian or a lion or
a What-not of the very last degree? Would you wear the
most striking clothes, give the richest dinners and buy the
longest press notices?

—W. E. B. DU BOIS
Criteria of Negro Art

EXHIBITIONS

Ticker tape rain
up in Harlem—
my welcome

felt like freedom
after the tuck-tail
of jail. The day's news

tossed at my feet
the stocks
bonds. Outside

I toured my bass
viol, upright,
playing by ear—wrestling

pythons—selling
ointments & appearances.
Even spoke to a klavern

of Ku Klux
on the golden rule.
Their ovation after

sounded like Spain
& France, the crowds
who applauded

when I fought foes
who never stood
a ghost

of a chance—Arthur Craven
poet & pugilist—
or 2 horses, charging,

held by my arms
padded, wrapped in steel
locks. With Paris

showgirls I showed
off my strength, hoisted
three at a time

over my rotting
smile. But polite
as she was Europa kept me

under her opera
glass—no surprise
a zeppelin only I could see

pursued me across London
with my white
Benz & wife

once the Great War
began. Between
sparring & bull

fights & my show
Seconds Out!
I offered to spy

for the States—or the highest
bidder—but the Continent kept on
serving me orders

to leave. Eviction.
Exile. I tired. Double
agent, ex-con

artist, champ
no longer, I retired
to the States that had tried

blindsiding me like my first
fight against the Giant
at the carny—come one

come all—pay
a worn nickel, win $5
—a fortune—if you last

3 rds. Still standing
by the 2d, I was
guided by the Giant

towards the tent
& his rube waiting
with a blackjack

—I put an end
to that. Quick. Left
his eye dark. Left

town to my own
applause
the way in 'fifteen

when Moran got a good one
in—though not
his Old Mary—

I clapped with my leather mitts
—congrats—
before—left arm broken—

my right broke his nose.
Freed, I had a fancy
to play Othello

—took a fourth
wife, white
—ended up

in film *False Nobility*
rolling my eyes
like cigars. I star

now in *Aida* as an Ethiopian
King. They have me
like Selassie, decked

out in skins. In stills
I bow—awkward—
to a blackface queen.

Do they put you
in chains?
"If they can get them

on me, okay & good,
but I got to show up
well—can't be

a ninny." *Do you yet*
know your fate?
"They take me up

to Memphis—not
Tenn., but the old
country—a prisoner. Boy,

I mean to struggle plenty."

It was on a hot day in Georgia when Jack Johnson drove into town. He was really flying: Zoooom! Behind his fine car was a cloud of red Georgia dust as far as the eye could see. The sheriff flagged him down and said, "Where do you think you're going, boy, speeding like that? That'll cost you $50!" Jack Johnson never looked up; he just reached in his pocket and handed the sheriff a $100 bill and started to gun the motor: ruuummm, ruummm. Just before Jack pulled off, the sheriff shouted, "Don't you want your change?" And Jack replied, "Keep it, 'cause I'm coming back the same way I'm going."

—WILLIAM H. WIGGINS, JR.
The Black Scholar

THE RACE { D. 10 JUNE 1945 }

Always was
ahead
of myself

my time.
Despised
by whites

& blacks alike
just cause
I didn't act right.

Gave Negroes
a bad name—
shame. Was

always a swinger
a fast talker—
my rights

the kind that broke
men's jaws.
Bigot laws.

Only good
Negro is dead
broke—if only you'd

bought less
cigars, suits
—they say—spent less

time chasing
ladies, racing
cars, goggles on

as if an aviator—
back when most
white men walked, not

to mention us. Some
nervous coloreds
half-hoped

I'd lose
so's not to prove
their race

superior
then act
like it—or not—

or out—or up-
pity, whatever
that means. The man

on the street
knows who
I am—no one's

Numidian, long
lost Caucasian
as whites claimed

once I won. I am pure
Caromontee stock.
Big bucks. I spent

my life fighting—
crossing color
lines I never drew

up, dreamt. I put
the race on
check—track—no Jack,

no Joe
Louis. My arms still
too short to go

gainst God—
on this last
road, old,

I will
speed, heading
not home

but to another
show & pot
of gold—too late

to see the truck
carrying what—
swerve—

"Remember
I was a man,
& a good one"—

in hospital
interns will think me
another fancy—

only the older doctor
shall know me—dying—
my Zephyr hugging

like an opponent
in the last round
this pole

of power—utility—
my black body
thrown free—

HOLLYWOOD AFRICANS { 1983 }

Basquiat paints

the town. PAW.
BWANA. SEVEN
STARS. Night

life—star-struck
Basquiat's arrived,
brought Toxic

& Rammellzee along
for the ride. Our trio
stomping new

ground—shaky,
kept. *Hills,*
that is—black

gold, Texas tea—
out west
Basquiat burns

his canvas ochre,
this trinity thin
as their ties. *Hip*

hop hippity hop—
Sunset Blvd
Walk of the Stars,

streets stretched
like limos. B
at last in the black,

dines out at Mr. Chow's.
IDI AMIN. 200 YEN.
Put it on his tab—

trading meals
for canvases free
loaded with msgs,

HERO-ISM.
TOBACCO in purple,
palimpsest. Toxic

& RMLZ cool, eyes
shaded by goggles,
hats with zs. Snores

ville. GANGSTERISM.
SELF-PORTRAIT
AS A HEEL #3. Hail,

hail, the gang's all
heels—no winners
or winters, just

wanderlust
amongst Oscars®
& MOVIE STAR

FOOTPRINTS
like an astronaut's.
Rock rock planet rock

don't stop—POP
CORN—SUGAR
CANE. Academy

Mammy Award
& another for Butler,
Rhett—To the moon

Jemima—PAW—
Basquiat rockets
NEW!—hands pressed

fresh into pavement,
permanent as a rap
sheet, booked.

ONION GUM { 1983 }

ONION GUM
MAKES YOUR
MOUTH TASTE

LIKE ONIONS
ONION GUM
MAKES YR MOUTH

TASTE LIKE ONIONS
INGREDIENTS:
ENRICHED FLOUR

Bunion gum makes
your mouth taste
like bunions

Bunion gum makes
your feet taste
like bunions

NIACIN, REDUCED IRON
Union gum
makes your

mouth taste
like Lincoln
Union gum

makes your mouth
head south
RIBOFLAVIN

engine engine
Injun gum
makes your

mouth taste
tobacco Injun
gum makes your

mouth taste
lottery
union gun

onion gun
Ink gum
makes your

mouth taste
calamari
Ink gum

makes your
mouth turn
negro

cuttle gum
colored gum
Bubble gum

makes yr mouth
pink & sore
Bubble gum

makes yr mouth
blow sugar
über gum

bazooka gum
THIAMINE
MONONITRATE

MADE IN JAPAN©
Redhot gum
makes yr mouth

taste like pepper
Redhot gum
makes yr mouth

taste like love
SNAKE
SERPENT

"HARMLSS"
ur-gum
anti-gum

ONION GUM
MAKES YR MOUTH
TASTE LIKE

ONIONS ONION
GUM MAKES
YOUR MOUTH

TASTE LK ONIONS

LANGSTON HUGHES

LANGSTON HUGHES
LANGSTON HUGHES
    O come now
    & sang
them weary blues—

Been tired here
feelin low down
    Real
      tired here
since you quit town

Our ears no longer trumpets
Our mouths no more bells
    FAMOUS POET©—
    Busboy—Do tell
us of hell—

Mr Shakespeare in Harlem
Mr Theme for English B
    Preach on
      kind sir
of death, if it please—

We got no more promise
We only got ain't
    Let us in
      on how
you 'came a saint

LANGSTON
LANGSTON
    LANGSTON HUGHES
    Won't you send
all heaven's news

CHARLIE CHAN ON HORN

For Prestige

Bird records
a few sides
(for contract

reasons) as Mr Charlie
Chan—no matter
the name his blues

sound the same,
same alto blaring
ALCHEMY,

licks exotic
as *Charlie Chan*
in Black Magic—

Chan's dark sidekick
Birmingham Brown
(a.k.a. Man-

tan Moreland)
seeing ghosts,
fleeing. *Feets*

do yo stuff—
THRIVING ON A RIFF,
Bird on a run

(in one place)
eyes bugged out
blowing

like Gabriel.
Solos snorted—
in one nose

& out the other.
Gone. Number one
son—don't they know

Charlie Chan
is a white man?
Fu Manchu too.

(Bless you.)
Parker play
your horn, not

no coon
no coolie in a white
suit. Bird's shot

his way to the top—
made a fist, tied off
& caught

the first vein
out of town.
Laying tracks—

NOWS THE TIME
NOWS THE TIME
BIRD GETS THE WORM—

Now dig
this—Basquiat
lit, lidded, does

a gravestone—
CPRKR
in the Stan-

hope Hotel,
the one Bird bit
the dust in (ON AIR)

high. TEETH.
HALOES
FIFTY NINE CENT.

Who knew how well
Basquiat would follow—
feet (six deep) first.

STARDUST

Lady sings
the blues
the reds, whatever

she can find—
short
changed, a chord—

God bless
the child
that's got his own

& won't mind
sharing some—
"BILLIES BOUNCE"

"BILLIES BOUNCE"
Miss Holiday's up
on four counts

of possession, three-
fifths, the law
—locked up—

licked—the salt
the boot—refused
a chance to belt

tunes in the clubs—
ex-con. Man,
she got it

bad—Brother
can you spare
a dime

bag? MEANDERING
WARMING UP
A RIFF—

she's all scat,
waxing—
SIDE A

SIDE B
OOH
SHOO DE

OBEE—
detoxed, thawed
in time

for Thanksgiving—live
as ammo, smoking
—NOV. 26 1945—

Day cold as turkey—

GODCHILD MILES DAVIS [*bonus track*]

Behind his father's house,
woodshedding—
head burning

TIN LEAD
ASBESTOS
like a conk—

THERE'S A RAINBOW ROUND
MY SHOULDER
THERE'S A SMALL HOTEL

THINGS AREN'T WHAT
      USED TO BE
THINGS TO COME—

locked in—
trying to kick
what's boiled

his veins—
SERUM CHOLESTOROL
CRUEL AZTEC GODS

HORSE PILL.
He's turned himself in
side out, traded cool

for cold
turkey, sweats.
1. A DRUNK

2. A LIAR
He's rid
of his reeds

like Moses in the bulrush
discovered, cover blown,
made a stepchild

adopted. TORY
TONCILLECTOMY
TOO BAD.

Left
in the dark
for days, visions—

THERE'S A FLATFOOT FOLLOWING ME
LINKY HE'S JUST
AROUND THE CORNER

GO GIVE HIM THE
ONE TWO.
Here, outside Saint

Louis, far
3. UNINHABITED BY WHITE MEN
from the scales

he climbs, sheds
like skin—
HORSE RACE TRACK©—

He's laid out
like a bet,
father

-ing himself—
giving birth to God
in a toolshed—

TRUMPET PLAYERS LAMENT, THE

UP AND ATOM
UPTOWN BLUES
US ON A BUS

CACTUS

CACTUS
Removed this stabbing
from his skin slow

as spit. Valve.
Heart.
A PISTOL VERSUS

A DINO
SAUR. He'll exit
3 days later

a new
known man—
clean. VI VIGOR

VO-DO-DO-DO-DE-O BLUES
WAITER AND THE PORTER

AND THE UPSTAIRS MAID
WATCH OUT (WATCHA TRYIN TO DO)—
His voice forever

hoarse, from one day
too soon after surgery
hollering

like a horn—WA WA WA
WELL GIT IT.
WE SHALL OVERCOME.

WELL YOU NEED'NT.

2005

RIDDLE ME THIS BATMAN

Doesn't everyone die
a dozen
times, ready

or not? ZLONK!
KAPOW! @;#$%*!?!
The cancer

slow, or sudden
as heart's failure—
desire desire—whether

suicide or mass
murder, we all
share final

breath. Rites.
Residuals.
To the Batetcetera

Robin! driving
crazy, the panicked
power pole he wraps

his car around—
is ours,
that last prayer, even

if only a shopping
list, some milky
thing. *Must*—

reach—
utility—
belt—too many

spinoffs in the works
too many arch-
villains going

makes things easy for.
HO HAHAHAAHAHAA
HEE—hear

them now.
Reruns. Side
kicks. So riddle

this, Batman—
with the water
in your tank rising

risen, the sharks
unfed, slandered
& anxious

what tricks lie up
your mask? what
geniusy grab-bag

will you open
after this word
from our sponsor?

LINK PARABOLE

Now back
to our show, to our
question marks & fish

hooks—what
suffering shark
repellent

Batty, what holy
torpedoes
will rescue you

high, dry?

RIDING WITH DEATH { 1988 }

The bit
of bones beneath
him, reined—

he mounts
Death
's bleached back—

a brown body out-
lined on linen.
SPINE. TORSO. SIN

HUESO. He's
too through
with this merry-

go-round—the clowns—
the giant stuffed
animals to win

or take your picture
with—the pony rides
& overpriced

food. *There's always
a unicycle.*
His hands turned

forks, tuning,
feeding what hunger
held him together

this long. Trawling
his own stomach.
Tripe. The snipe hunt

he's begun has come
up empty—left holding
the bag—trick,

nickel—this cat's
gotten out, crossed
the path. Curious—

his horse
turned back
from our foxhunt,

this possum run.
Given in—SAMO©
AS AN ESCAPE

CLAUSE—found face
down
like a payment.

And we who for ages
whaled, blubber
& wonder

why he's thrown
ashore, rowed
himself here

hallelujah—answered
out the blue
whale some unseen

call. A siren—
the ambulance
racing a sea

of cars—*emergency*—
family only
beyond this

point—our fists
against his breath-
less chest.

EROICA { 1988 }

BEAM: TO LOOK
BEAN: TO SUN
BAT: AN OLD OLD

WOMAN
MAN DIES.
MAN DIES.

AIRCOOLED
CONDENSER
BAGPIPE: 1940S

VACUUM CLEANER
B.O.A.C. : BUREAU
OF DRUG ABUSE

CONTROL
BALE OF STRAW: WHITE
BLOND FEMALE

BALL & CHAIN: WIFE
BALLOON ROOM:
PLACE WHERE

MARIJUANA IS SMOKED
MAN DIES. MAN
DIES. MAN DIES.

BALLS: TESTICLES
BAM: (FROM BAMBITA)
BANANA: ATTRACTIVE

LIGHT SKIN
BLACK FEMALE
BAND: WOMAN

BAND: JAZZ
BANG: INJECTION
OF NARCOTICS

OR SEX.
MAN DIES.
BANJO: INSTR

FRM WEST
AFRKA
BANK: TOILET

TNT
(—6H2 CH)
MORNING GLORY

SWEET POTATO
MAN DIES.
MAN—

FOR BLUES
FIXIN TO DIE
BLUES

BARK: HUMAN SKIN

SHRINE OUTSIDE BASQUIAT'S STUDIO, SEPTEMBER 1988

Back on Great
Jones
his face

against the façade
fronting the carriage
house rented

from Warhol—
inside, his suits
stiffen from starch,

spilt paint.
He's bought
the farm whole,

enchilada
& all—August
& the heat

covering everything,
needle-sharp,
asleep. No more

feeding
his habit art—
he's gone

& done it
this time, taken
his last dive.

Exit, stage right.
A broken
record—his black

skin thick,
needled
into song—

a swan's. Upon
graffitied brick—
INSIDIOUS MENACE

LANDLORD
TENANT—
folks pile

candles flowers
photos notes
to God & lace—

anything TO REPEL
GHOSTS, keep
his going at bay

before memory comes
early, snarling
& sweeps him

into the mouth
of euphemism—
sanitation worker, waste

management engineer,
garbage man, dumpster
diver, trash

heap, heaven.

HENRY GELDZAHLER: *You got rid of your telephone a while ago. Was that satisfying?*

J-M BASQUIAT: Pretty much. Now I get all these tele-grams. It's fun. You never know what it could be. "You're drafted," "I have $2,000 for you." It could be anything. And because people are spending more money with telegrams they get right to the point. But now my bell rings at all hours of the night. I pretend I'm not home . . .

Making It New

URGENT TELEGRAM TO JEAN-MICHEL BASQUIAT

HAVENT HEARD FROM YOU IN AGES STOP LOVE YOUR
LATEST SHOW STOP THIS NO PHONE STUFF IS FOR BIRDS
LIKE YOU STOP ONCE SHOUTED UP FROM STREET ONLY

RAIN AND YOUR ASSISTANT ANSWERED STOP DO YOU
STILL SLEEP LATE STOP DOES YOUR PAINT STILL COVER
DOORS STOP FOUND A SAMO TAG COPYRIGHT HIGH

ABOVE A STAIR STOP NOT SURE HOW YOU REACHED STOP
YOU ALWAYS WERE A CLIMBER STOP COME DOWN SOME
DAY AND SEE US AGAIN END

RETROSPECTIVE

I met Jean-Michel Basquiat a few days before he died.
Before or after, it doesn't really matter.
—DANY LAFERRIÈRE

In the dark, the nasty
night, mother of million
nights, you return

looking, not for fame
but ducats, not begging
but collecting

on what was
owed you, getting back
what you sharked.

Lien.
Let us guess
JMB—you can see

everything clear
as your complexion,
as composed. COWARDS

WILL GIVE
TO GET RID
OF YOU. Even when

your skin gave in
to the heroin, you still
looked young & beautiful—

yet you confess
you feel much
better now, got

a handle on things,
the drugs fled on
out, left cold

turkey. THE SKY
IS THE LIMIT©.
Wings

& white meat.
Spleen still
missing, but not

quite missed.
If only
you'd said so

long like a television
station, signed off
the air—Star

Spangled Banner
blowing before bars—
red, yellow,

more—color—
before brief
black—the static—

from

jelly roll

{ A B L U E S }

(composed & arranged by)

kevin young

{ **2003** }

I love my baby
But my baby don't love me

I love my baby wooo
My baby don't love me

I really loves that woman
Can't stand to leave her be

A-ain't but one thing
Makes Mister Johnson drink

I gets low bout how you treat me baby
I begin to think

Oh babe
Our love won't be the same

You break my heart
When you call Mister So & So's name

{ ROBERT JOHNSON }

EPITHALAMION

Before the world
was water, just
before the fire

or the wool,
was you—
yes—your hands

a stillness—
a mountain. Marry
me. Let the ash

invade us & the ants
the aints—
let—my God—

the anger
but do not answer
No—such stars

shooting, unresolved
are about to be ours—
if we wish. Yes—

the course, the sail
we've set—our mind—
leaves no wake

just swimming sleep.
Stand
& I will be born

from your arm—
a thing eagled, open,
above the unsettled,

moon-made sea.

CAKEWALK

Baby, you make
me want

to burn up all
my pies

to give over
an apple to fire

or loose track
of time & send

a large pecan
smokeward, or

sink some peach
cobbler. See, to me

you are a Canada
someplace north

I have been, for years,
headed & not

known it.
If only I'd read

the moss on the tree!
instead of shaking

it for fruit—
you are a found

fallen thing—
a freedom—not this red

bloodhound ground—

DIXIELAND

I want the spell
of a woman—her

smell & say-so—
her humid

hands I seek—zombied—
The bayou

of my blood—standing
water & the 'squitoes

all hungry—*hongry*—
to see both our bodies

knocked out—dragged
quicksand down—

They'll put up posters—
have you seen—all over town—

Days later we'll be drug
naked from the swamp

that is us—re-
suscitated, rescued—

the cops without one clue.

DITTY

You, rare as Georgia
snow. Falling

hard. Quick.
Candle shadow.

    The cold
spell that catches

us by surprise.
The too-early blooms,

tricked, gardenias blown about,
circling wind. Green figs.

    Nothing stays. I want
to watch you walk

the hall to the cold tile
bathroom—all

        night, a lifetime.

EARLY BLUES

Once I ordered a pair of shoes
But they never came.

RAGTIME

Like hot food
I love you

like warm
bread & cold

cuts, butter
sammiches

or, days later, after
Thanksgiving

when I want
whatever's left

BOASTS

Wouldn't be no fig leaf
if I was Adam

but a palm tree.

————————

Once I danced all
night, till dawn

& I—who never
did get along—

decided to call a truce—
my body

buckets lighter,
we shook hands

& called it blues.

————————

Mama, I'm the man
   with the most

biggest feet—
   when I step out

my door to walk the dog
   round the block

I'm done.

SONG OF SMOKE

To watch you walk
cross the room in your black

corduroys is to see
civilization start—

the *wish-*
whish-whisk

of your strut is flint
striking rock—the spark

of a length of cord
rubbed till

smoke starts—you stir
me like coal

and for days smoulder.
I am no more

a Boy Scout and, besides,
could never

put you out—you
keep me on

all day like an iron, out
of habit—

you threaten, brick-
house, to burn

all this down. You leave me
only a chimney.

ERRATA

Baby, give me just
one more hiss

We must lake it fast
morever

I want to cold you
in my harms

& never get lo

I live you so much
it perts!

Baby, jive me gust
one more bliss

Whisper your
neat nothings in my near

Can we hock each other
one tore mime?

All light wrong?

Baby, give me just
one more briss

My won & homely

You wake me meek
in the needs

Mill you larry me?

Baby, hive me just
one more guess

With this sing
I'll thee shed

PLAYER PIANO

On the sun-starched
deck of a fishing boat

I have watched fish flip-flop

helpless as a heart—
thwap-thwap, thwap-

thump—and wished
to be caught

just like that,
a keeper. Mouth

that won't quit moving—

Afternoons I wander aisle
after aisle in the bookstore, leafing

through women's magazines
to see if my name

lists among diseases
on slick pages marked Your Health,

How to Spot a Cheat,
the latest from Spain.

Please quit lying

to someone else, save all
your stories for me—

This afternoon I tore out
cards for perfume

grew lightheaded

and thought of you—overwhelmed
yet drawn near, the way bees

can smell fear—then smeared
competing scents

over the thin
skin inside my wrists.

Don't mind the cheating
I mind the leaving—

For days I've felt
sick. My stomach

a-swim, a ship
tossing. Think

of you two together
and the day I will pop in

to pick up whatever
I left: unlit

candles, underwear
folded neat and bleached

white as a flag of peace.
Driving home,

feel the quease of days,
my car's lingering reek

till I reach under
and find the offender—

under my seat, out of sight—

an apple, uneaten except
by time and heat. The rest

forgot, wrapped in rot. Soon
I'll teach my hands

better, how to roll over
to beg—

For now, chucking that husk
away, I think of stones

thrown into the sea,
how still

for you I would churn
its salt to taffy.

LOCOMOTIVE SONGS

We were hobos every year.
It was cheap—

Our mother each
Halloween smudged our cheeks

stuffed us in someone
else's clothes—

We hopped houses
like trains

asking for sweets

Much like last night,
empty-armed, at your door

I begged you

————

Tonight the train horn
sounds like plenty

enough loud
to warm even the autumn—

The night air with a nip
that catches by surprise—

White light, blue
light, fog starting to rise

————

She has me tied,
a tongue, to the tracks

Her new man's
elaborate moustache

Train comin fast

Can't cry
out to save my life

Drats

———————

I've heard tell
of a town where the train

bound for New Orleans slows
just enough, a turn

that folks place cars
good only for insurance in—

The train cashes them
coming round the bend—too late

to stop, to slow to derail—
That's how I feel

watching you & the station
being pulled away, one hand

hovering the emergency brake
the other

out to wave

AUTUMN SONG

Even a dog got him
a house.

     Me, I am rent

unpaid, or late—
I am a small bird

beneath a big wheel.
Snail-brown

of November. Night.

     Even a bird-dog knows
     what way is home.

Me, I hunted
the high places, the low

where only the wingless go.

     Of the trees, nests
     are all that's left—

in wind pine limbs creak
like an old man's,

a door opening.
The noise beneath my feet!

     Even a bird,
     a dog, got him a cage

he can bark
all night in, or sing.

BUSKING

The day folds up like money
if you're lucky. Mostly

sun a cold coin
drumming into the blue

of a guitar case. Close
up & head home.

Half-hundred times I wanted
to hock these six strings

or hack, if I could, my axe
into firewood. That blaze

never lasts.
I've begged myself hoarse

sung streetcorner
& subway over a train's blast

through stale air & trash.
You've seen me, brushed past—

my strings screech
& light up like a third rail—

Mornings, I am fed by flies,
strangers, sunrise.

from **SLEEPWALKING PSALMS**

Verde que te quiero verde.
—LORCA

I.

Every day since I have practiced a sort
of amnesia, forgetting keys, misplaced
names. I have begun to escort
spiders out of doors, into wind, unrest

reaching them at last. Even then
you rise up, remembered—a polaroid
or slip of paper where your writing's begun
to fade. Black, turned brown. I try to avoid

spring, but dust rises and settles over
all things, even the words like
ours, *his* and *hers,* who stole the covers
all seem so far. Green again. Schwinn bike

in the garage I'll never ride, three-speed,
its thick chain locked. You gone with the key.

3.

Soon I'll thank you for leaving
all at once, and for good—
no more months of begging,
or not, of waiting for what

we both know only grows,
goes away—our nights days
we'd lie beside the other awake,
pretending sleep, sorrow

a child snoring between us, slightly,
child we'll never have. Thank you
then, for not even the note, just my
opening the door to find you

missing, like my fortune cookie
our now-final meal, broke open empty.

    5.
When I said I didn't mind
your leaving I lied—
even the funny-lookingest kid
in class gets a valentine

and I hear he's now got mine.
These nights I've become
caged by quiet, a zoo of one—
a polar bear pacing like tide

his half-empty pool, loopy from heat,
coat grown green—or some lust-
lost captive who won't quite mate,
so his keeper brings in a stud to save

the breed. Or so, unkept, you claim.
Tell me his name.

    6.
Stumbling home in last night's
smoke-soaked hair and clothes,
strip bars all closed
and wanting to call you right

away, to plead and preen.
I try sleep instead. The phone
can't even recall your voice, no
more your name on my machine.

Lord, let me never drink booze
at least for one more week.
Lord, let me eat more fruit
than comes in a mixed drink.

No one answers
where you are.

   7.
There are no more saints—
only people with pain
who want someone to blame.
Or praise.

I am one of them, of course.
Miracle, or martyr, or worse—
wanting a desert to crawl
out into, marking my fall

by sun and thirst
instead of by this silence
that swims over me. Oasis
not really there, penitence—

you the sand I've crawled across,
my hairshirt, my tiny albatross.

CHORALE

Quite difficult, belief.
Quite terrible, faith

that the night, again,
will nominate

you a running mate—
that we are of the elect

& have not yet
found out. That the tide

still might toss us up
another—what eyes

& stars, what teeth!
such arms, alive—

someone we will, all
night, keep. Not

just these spiders
that skitter & cobweb,

share my shivering bed.

SLIDE GUITAR

Tonight I wake with mud
in my head, a thick

brown I sink
my line into. Fists

full of fish.
Tonight even the storm

cannot calm me.

My hands tonight scatter
about the place, folded

quiet like fine lady's gloves.
Cue the saddish music—

how like flies it rises!

Outside, the suicides
float by buoyant

in their lead balloons.

REQUIEM

Your name is harm.
The bar fills

& empties eddies
like a drink & is not

the answer. Ain't—
I'm all kinds

of lost, watered,
down. The shot

glass like
a microscope strong.

I should be a natn'l
day of mourning

one week minus
mail. Entire month

of Sunday—a sabbath
swaying

mouthing hymns—
Where, pray

tell, went the words?
Rider, you are a whole

church-worth of hurt—

vows

My wife of words,
ambassador of grief.

From you I am far,
firefly fading, jarred.

Across the night lawn
lightning bugs wed.

Through woods echoes
my widowed voice.

EVENSONG

At dusk women
walking alone give off

the strangest light—
till you realize they're not—

a dark dog races
to meet one, leash

tailing; or,
a boyfriend not worth

the wait, gleeful
ungraceful, follows

far too close.
Children tire of ignoring

their mothers who half-watch
them holler. The boys

skateboarding beyond
even their bodies

have got it right—

fling yourselves, friends,
into whatever guardrail or concrete

the world has, then find
someone to get it all

down on tape.
Later, the falls will

seem obvious, about
to happen—re-wound,

the women all look
better off—and those

who fall shall stay

airborne, oblivious, halfway
to happy.

PARLOR SONG

      I spider the days—
each one a shorter

stitch in the quilt
which you will kick off the bed

quickly, when you return.
Dawn—

patchwork once—
is now these scraps

all day I save & make
something out of

that the dark undoes.

———————

      You & your travels!
your encyclopedias

have kept me keeping

company with the quiet.
Outside

my window the suitors circle, smoke

their unfiltereds
into ash. They ask

after me.
They serenade,

guitars in hand, play
their second

fiddle. After you
they ask also

> interested

Are you dead—

Have I any word—

> I repeat—

You have taken afield

your samples to sell & soon
we'll see you scraping your boots

along this very stoop.

———————

The dog, greying, has grown

too tired to hunt
the underbrush, to rise

& whine whenever
the wind our screen

door creaks.
> At night I dream

your skin quicksand,
ground that gives

way—sinks—

I wake alone.
Come home
    & warm

your side of the wrought
iron bed

I've kept for you cool.

—————

    For you my list of things
to fix will be nil

though the old place you will

barely know—it's too much
the same as that day

you whistled out our door
with your nicotine

promises & schemes
of green.

    Our old photos
fading, the piano

unplayed, your fingerprints
cover the mirrors

as does dust. All night
I toss

like the scattered stars you steer
somewhere by, shore

to shore, hawking your
insurance
      & whiskey.

THRENODY

Even cars have their graveyards,
piled and turning

the one color
of after—

And me with nowhere
to send my bones

to be counted,
made whole.

This is
Providence, Providence—

Not even a dentist to visit
once a year like an aunt

squeezing my cheeks
too tight.

Without you I got no one
to say *sorry* to—

Only this winter
pretending spring, fooling

few blooms. *New*
Haven, next—

The trees never do reach
our train that clatters past

blurring cars—three parts
primer, the rest rust—

the color of ash,
of ember.

COTILLION

Tonight I am a man
tap-dancing the train tracks

red light—red—
while the 10:50 nears,

sweet horn blowing.
I jitterbug,

Charleston bound—
take down

the tarnished stars, my breath
will shine them up new.

Tonight I want a tongue
stuck to the wintry track

& swear when that freight train comes
I'll yank my thick head back.

Tonight I'll grab hold
the striped arm

of the crossing bar—
let it dance me

round real slow.

Tonight I tango
alone.

LATE BLUES

If
      I die,
let me

be buried
      standing—
I never lied

to anyone,
      or down—
wouldn't want

to start up now.

LITANY

The dirt grows up
around us, dear,
the dank & the way down

of it. The day.
Once I was
in love. Once I would not say

or could not, the under
that awaits.
Today, I say over

your one name,
sound
that sole gravity.

———————

The old draw-
bridge, rusted, is always up

———————

North, New
London—we cross
ourselves & the river

into the past—
the submarine
memorial for those lost

at sea, sunk
miles under—the docks dry—
the rust & mist

———————

Count me among the missing

———————

The apples
have not kept

their promises,
grown rotten

& ran, skins
bled into brown

———————

I come to your town
fog clinging to bridges
to the baring branches

———————

In the calamitous city
in the songs & sinners
among the thousand throngs

I barter & belong. Out
of the coward's tooth
& arms of ocean

out of sheer
contrariness
I continue. Keep watch.

———————

Hunger has me
by the belly

————————

Why does the waiting
scare you & me
the silence that surrounds

it, us, this life—

I am inside this
stone you call
a city. I am king

of the gypsies.

Thin throne air.
No crown to speak of.
My body

dying, divine.

————————

The day will, I know,
come—not now—
but soon & they will say

you are gone

Will I know it by
the lack of breath
—mine—the long grief
in the trees

Or will it be you
they tell of me—sickened,
stiffened, through.
Do not

worry. Will be
me beside the foot
of your bed, nothing

haunting, just
a hint. A wish.
Think

of me & breathe!
say over
again my many

my million names.

ELEGY, NIAGARA FALLS

for Bert King, d. 1996

Here snow starts
but does not
stick—stay—

is not enough
to cover
the bare thaw-

ed ground.
Grief is the god
that gets us—

good—in the end—
Here—churches
let out

early—in time
to catch the lunch
special—at my local

hotel. Sunday—
even the bus
boy has your

face. And still
having heard
some days later you

were dead—
I haven't caught
sight—day

or night—
of the Falls. I know
they are somewhere—

near—like you—all
gravity & fresh water
& grace rushing through—

CHAMBER MUSIC

JELLY ROLL OUTTAKES

{ **1999–2004** }

DUET

Sarah & Jeff's Wedding
6 November 2004

Let us begin
by being free.

Then, to know just
what we need—

Night without
a light

The dark
full of dream.

And you & I, I
& you, & all

the letters in between.

HURRICANE SONG

Lady, won't you wait
out the hurricane

all night at my place—
we'll take cover like

the lamps & I'll
let you oil

my scalp. Please, I needs
a good woman's hands

caught in my hair, turning
my knots to butter.

All night we'll churn.
Dawn

will lean in too soon—
you'll leave out into

the wet world, winded
& alone, knowing

the me only
midnight sees.

FLAMENCO

How I know
happiness is this

sadness in
the fruit of it—

To think
you were to me dead

once I did not know
you & now

the bloom of you—
yes'm—fills

my mouth!
Happy has me

round the throat—
throttled—& won't let go

SAETA

The martyr is borne
through town on the backs

of believers.
Such a ghost ship!

all skull, ragged sails.
Your arms arrows—

I quiver

& am unwell.
Touching you I heal

places I never knew
needed.

If faith this is not
do not let me know.

You my splinter,
my swath of bone.

CHAMBER MUSIC

WOODWIND:
This morning your mouth
Was all I could think about

FIDDLE:
Like a violin you leave
The sweetest

Bruise just beneath
My chin.

UPRIGHT BASS:
Love that place
Where your hip hits

Your waist
& my head fits

Perfect, rests
Like music

SLIDE TROMBONE:
All day that scent
In the crook

Of your neck
Distracts

HORNS:
Woke early, the light
Blues all in my bed

Where I wish
You warmed instead.

RHYTHM SECTION:
Without you the room
Grown small—

Only then can I see
How each night we rocked

A steady groove
Where the headboard

Hugged the wall.

STRAYS

The moon of you
I want to meet—

faraway, waning.

————————

Asleep in the sun
of your arms

then cold
when you're gone.

————————

In the dark where we
can no longer see

I want your hands blurry
over me, reading

the braille of my body.

————————

Your narcotic touch.
Your such & such

makes me rush
home through dark

slick streets & hush
to our bright

too-hot house—only you
sleep somewhere else.

I miss you like a monument
misses its dead—

the stone heads
staring, the hands

stiff, or still,
half-eroded

by time. Tell me
& I'll write what you want

near my name

ELECTION DAY

Storm me.
Send

me down into the dirt
& dark, raise

me like thunder up.
Show me the sun

of your legs open.
Shine.

Let our shadows
spill into

each other, let
our souls

brighten
& become one.

Let our bones break
into song.

SONG OF FALL

That year the crops shouldered
the sky & our bellies stayed

so full we never
knew hunger:
a hound dog

hanging round
the front porch
begging whatever

we tossed under.
It stayed summer.
We worked the days long

till our hands
burned bone, were bruise
—his & mine—

then all night touched
lightly in the heat.
Kissed

his scarred side.
We named each other's bodies
with what few words

we had need of.
Morning always arrived
too soon

lost in skin's rain—
he'd kiss my eyes awake.

So, that evening—
        my man out
by the barn, the lowing—

        sun like a beehive
fallen, broken open
        & spilling honey—

I almost didn't hear
        the knock
despite our small house, lost

        in my own mind.
But there it was
        again, the Salesman

with his song, his hello
        offering up
quick crops

or a cleaner better
        than any other,
some pitch

        to get rich.
Hissed
        his promises

into my ears
        which hadn't known pearls
or rings—

        which suddenly felt naked
as we were those nights
        I plumb forgot

to be ashamed. *No,*
        I said through the screen,
Thank you—

But he stood at my door
        asking was I covered—
he was selling

        Life, which of course
meant Death, meant
        What If.

Long had I lived
        without thought
of after—our days

long, the dark
        you could walk
without worry. But that Salesman

        in his shiny
suit, the jacket he shed like skin

said otherwise, showed
        me lists & pictures
& my own

        carelessness—
he promised us a plot
        where together

my man & I could be buried
        beneath an apple tree.
I had thought we would live

as lovers forever—
never thought of wife
or father or the future—

But now I saw
it everywhere: hunger
is what held

the world together, kept
the moon married
to water

& the dog barking
in need of company.

All at once the fields
seemed silent
as God—

The ground red
& hard
like my hands—

The soil suddenly
turned to rust
& I wanted to be richer

than it was—
so I signed.
The Salesman's smile

a dotted line.
And like that,
he was gone.

Soon the children
        arrived, their mouths
that needed filling—

        the crops began
balding—the dog whining—
        & I began to salt

away money
        like pork. But no matter
how much we smoked

        & kept, it never
was enough.
        Everywhere, hunger:

the children needing
        new things, & we
growing old of each other—

        And the rain
remembered to fall,
        & the fall

remembered to rain—
        autumn turned
to red mud

& our clothes, new, to stain.

BLACK MARIA

FROM

BLACK MARIA

being the adventures of

DELILAH REDBONE & A.K.A. JONES

POEMS PRODUCED *and* DIRECTED BY

KEVIN YOUNG

{ 2005 }

BLACK MARIA

{RHYMES WITH PARIAH}

slang meaning a police wagon

or hearse

THE SET-UP

Snake oil sales
were slow. So I hung

out my shingle on
a shadow.

Desk-drawer liquor

A dead man's loan. Soon
chinless stoolies

slunk & doorjambed—
ratted

that she ain't no
good, that she wears a watch

on both wrists. Too
many midnights.

Evidence mounting like butterflies

Still I made them informants
for phonies, phoned

to hear her breath.
She was faith

enough to believe.
She's a peach. A pistol.

I waived my fee

I left my agency

Came home to rooms ran-
sacked, tossed

by invisible hands.
Hip flask. Blackjacked.

Swig,
mickey slip, slug.

I woke doubled & crossed

Drug, ferried
through whisky alleys

Bruisers, suicide doors

The crooked chief interrogated
me about her body

She's no more mine, no eye
witness, nor alibi

No one will attest she ever
did exist.

I was her autumn guy

By the wharf was left
waterlogged & wise

My dogs dead
tired, I humped it

home, humming gumshoe blues.

THE CHASE

I didn't have a rat's chance.
Soon as she walked in in

That skin of hers
violins began. You could half hear

The typewriters jabber
as she jawed on: *fee, find, me,*

poor, please.
Shadows & smiles, she was.

Strong scent of before-rain

Her pinstripe two-lane
legs, her blackmail menthol.

She had all the negatives

Hidden safe
& would not reveal the place.

Before you could say
denouement, I was on her case—

Slant hat, broad
back, my entrenched coat

Of fog. Fleabags,
neon blinds undrawn—

The foreshadows fell on her face.

All night I tailed, staked
the joint. Found

Her with the butler
playing patty-cake.

Baker's man. She nurse
him like beer

Till dawn. Doozy.
Was from her woozy,

My eyes wet.
Binocular mist.

I took two to the chest

Was all
rain, her blurring face

Her snuffed, stubbed-out
lipstuck cigarette.

SPEAKEASY

The band vamped,
sunlight leaving—sequined,

Delilah Redbone swung
her hardships & sang—

Sporting my lucky
hundred-proof cologne

I listened hard at the bar
as the houselights dimmed—

Rich widows passed matches
with messages in the flaps

Weary husbands with ring-
worn hands sweated

Like their drinks, getting up
the nerve to ask.

I tossed a few back

The band cranked, sharp,
trumpet neath a hat—

Glasses & dance
cards empty, ladies winked

For a light so often
—*Say, mister*—

You'd think you were
the election-year mayor

Handing out favors.
Every joe here

Named John or Jack
or Hey You or Doe—

My answer, mostly, *No.*

Another round & the band
blew its medley midnight

Husbands hugged
their mistresses tighter

And she scat till the moon
caught itself

In the trees like a balloon
let go by a child, crying,

At the county fair.
My saltwater

Shotglass. My flask

Full of lighter fluid.
The piano boogied twilight

She sang & swooned & the sun
started up

An argument with what was left
of the dark—

The swingshift stumbled out

The graveyard drug in thirsty
& worse. Delilah sang on

About hearts that break like high-note
glass—or jaws—

That break more than men
in the mob-run union.

The band beat louder
passing a hat, damping

Foreheads with *uh-huhs*
& handkerchiefs

While Miss Redbone sang:

Lord, I'm afraid
Whoa, so afraid

I done married Mud
& took on his name.

THE OFFICE

His diploma from Hard
Knocks College

Hung there askew.
His cologne—

Smelling salts—filled
the messy room.

The name on his lambskin
scrawled in Pig Latin.

No heat—
except what steamed

Between us—
his breath blew rings.

My uncomfortable
underthings.

My eyebrows
plucked apostrophes

Making him mine.

Like a heart my feet ached
after climbing the steep stairs

In skyscraper heels
to his semi-suite. His assistant—

Miss McGuffin—
buzzed me in.

I talked circles
round him, his bachelor's

Degree in bourbon
& silence served

Him well. What
I gave him: The Soft

Sell. The Hard Luck Tale.
The Runaround. The Quick

Take. The Hayseed.
The Switcheroo. The Second Guess

& Third Degree.

The lights flickered
on & off, the street.

He lit another stogie—

I never did mind his cigars,
their peat, though most thought

They reeked
of horses in the field.

Honestly, that hint
of home is what

I'd missed—
He was biscuits

& figs, was sweet
potato pie cooling

On the sill. Suddenly,
the somewhere I had to be

Went away—
I even wanted to reveal

My real name.

Instead, sweated
in the cold.

Like an old lady
at the matinee

I popped a noisy mint
as if that would help me

Not breathe mist—

My threadbare fur.
My secondhand

Story. Still, for me
he'll fall like Jericho's walls—

You see, he still believed
in something—

Even if it was me,
his losing big-bet team.

I'll quick cure
him of that.

I tried telling him
my maiden name was Trouble

But even that was too much
like a touch

Of perfume behind my ear,
my neck & knees,

That he needed to get near
Just to be sure . . .

His hair dark
as a sparrow's tail

That soon I'll sprinkle
with salt & grey

So he'll never fly away.

THE HUSH

For those few nights
we were husband & wife—

Mister & Missus
Smith was the name

we registered under,
laughing ourselves low.

Let the busybody bellboy stare.

I didn't care—
all night Mister Smith's arms

were long enough
to reach round me

& touch—to lift up
& threshold me

to the buckling bed.
There was no one else

in the joint,
it felt, just us knocking

the paint-by-numbers
pictures aslant, ordering up

whatever food they had—
some paper-bag gin—

I didn't care—
pulled the pins

like a grenade's
from my hair

& let the flowers
wilt behind my ear.

Let whisky weather
my throat

& still tomorrow I'll sing—

Let the weather
spill its liquor

wherever it wants.
I'll sink

to that. Who cares
what the world went on

doing—those few nights
& lies & sneaky-pete wine

that made us newlyweds
made sense—

Those nights the only rings

we owned
were those we left behind

from drinks sweating
on the warped wood,

our wobbly vanity.

THE ALIAS

Bruised like gin
stirred too quick

Ruining the tonic

I stumbled home
put on a steak eye-patch

& fixed me another drink
hoping this one would take

The way she never did.
On the rocks

& stiff. Alls
I got left—

A key to a safe
deposit that's empty

& one lousey alias—
S.O.S. Mallone.

(My real name's
A.K.A. Jones.

Leastwise
that's what I been told.)

Hey buddy, welcome home—

Murphy bed like a booby
trap, springs shot

My mattress thin as the bills
I once stuffed it with.

I drink a lot
about my thinking problem—

Nightcap,
noontime nip—

She my unquit habit.

This roof with more
leaks than I

Could ever fix, buckets
of rusty rainwater I bend

Low to drink. Brimming over,

My good eye watched
all night the storm

Drown the street in worms

STILLS

With her, guilty
was my only plea.

✳

When we kiss, her leg kicks
up like a chorus line!

✳

The next day what awaits: flat fizz,
an ache cured only by bitters.

✳

Two eggs,
over queasy.

✳

Chew fat. Spit
blood. Gargle peroxide. Repeat.

✳

She's pro
bono, a quid pro.

✳

I've given, like gin,
her up, again.

✳

Even my shadow
has me followed.

STILLS

When we met, her first request:
Got a light?

✱

I only had dark
so gave her that instead.

✱

Once I looked rose-colored;
now I see only red.

✱

Her cigarettes burn
along just one side:

✱

Someone else thunk
bout her all the time.

✱

On my door I hung a sign:
GONE WISHING. BACK IN 5.

✱

Ashtray full of butts
& maybes.

✱

The echo of her heels down the hall
to me means reveille.

THE SUSPECTS

Threatening rain

The boozy,
overdressed dame

with a voice to match

The unbent bootblack

The one-armed pickpocket
with a nose

for the horses
Informant shot in his tracks

Pullman porter
with a chemistry degree

A well-minxed martini

Last of the light

Too much shadow
around the eyes

Newshound nosing round
the place

Throat cut
like a phone line

An assignation
The asinine accomplice

Here comes the bribe

The day player
who flubs his line

The prizefighter's
blackmail fall

Mousey majorette
at the used bookstore

who unbuttons her hair
& lets down her blouse

Misplaced lightning

Face full of smoke

Character actor
whose accent changes more

than a leading lady's wardrobe

The once-over
The okie-doke

The moon a thumb-
print pressed

in the black police book
kept by the night

Put your hands
where I can see em

Cryptic telegram

Slow cigar ash

And Death, the well-
dressed doorman,

his pockets stuffed with cash.

THE BOSS

Even his walking
stick was crooked.

He didn't need it,
or me, he'd say—let me

know he kept us both
for show. His hands

clean as a cop's whistle,
nails filed

to toothpicks. Slick—
he taught me

to kiss, & silence,
how to tell tons

just from the eyes.
His were ice

picks, raised,

or icebergs tearing
into the berth

of some *Titanic*.
Watch em sink.

He was never in between—
either gargantuan

or thin
as a lie. He sharpened

knives on other men's spines.
He hated losing

even a dime, would bet
the farm, then steal

from the till. Weed em
& reap.

He treated me
like his money—took me

out only
when he needed something

& fast.
Even his toupee—

imported, real
human hair—was one-sided

& levitated
above his head like a lightbulb

burned dim.
No wonder when

that detective stumbled in—

smelling of catharsis
& cheap *ennui,*

begging to be
given an extra week

with his knees—
I wanted him like nobody's

business. His
blown kiss.

Never laundered
like money, that dick's suit

stayed rumpled like the pages
of a paperback dropped

in the tub, drowned, the end
you read first to find out

whodunit, never
mind why.

THE GUNSEL

Armed like his teeth

Nervous as a thief
at the cop convention

A ballerina before
a buffet

He laughed loud
& overlong

At The Boss Man's jokes—
again, the one about the senator

& the nun. Something
about bad habits . . .

His were spitting
& cursing, a fondness

For the edge of things:
towns, skirts, a drizzle

That seemed to fall
only when least fitting,

Or most. Love scenes
& holdup schemes.

*

He smoked for show,
kept the top dog's highball

Full a ice like
chewed glass. Kept his own

Brass knuckles polished
by breath & sweat—

His walk favored his left

Ever since that incident
with the mayor's wife

& two full flights
had gimped his right.

❋

Squirrelly, he kept quiet & his eye
on me always—sideways

He watched me that summer
I made the swimming pool

My bedside table, the moon
my chaperone—

Was paid to see if my heart hurried
when I saw that detective

Slur & slink his way into the room.

But toss a few smiles, maybe a strut,
his way & that guard

Dog would turn lap dog—
he'd fetch & beg but never stay—

Knew neither would I.

❋

The day I did split
my beau The Boss was out

Cold, KO'd by drink

Wearing my stocking
as a cap & snoring

The symphony in Z.

I stuffed my hatbox
full, left only perfume

Littering the room.
Despite the echo

between his ears, that flunky
heard me, the stairs creaky

As his bones. Don't know why

That hired fist let me
walk, a head start, while

He & the night watched—

Just spat his shoes
till they shone

Like exclamation points,
said *See youse*

& wished me dead
& luck.

STILLS

We undress shy
as a gun.

＊

The mailman's son, I am
nor snow, nor night, nor gloom.

＊

Her eyelashes long
& false as an alarm.

＊

He say, she say,
foreplay, amscray.

＊

Her cocktail dress pours
over my bare floor.

＊

Her feather boa
hissing yes.

＊

Without her I am incomplete—
prehensible, licit, couth.

＊

Wisdom this tooth
aching I want removed.

NIGHT CAP

He loves me slow
as gin, then's out

light-switch quick.
The moon's burned-

out bulb in a blackened sky,
I lie in the dark & want

his name to be mine—
or to be alone—

Wish I could walk out
this overheated railroad flat

& everyone on the street
knew me, home, & he'd wake

in bed alone & wonder
where I'd gone. Instead,

his unsteady snore—
calling the hogs, sawing.

Sleep, for now, is almost
enough—want it to start

in my toes & tingle
upward, then explode

behind my eyes, closed—
Said start down in my toes

& explode behind
eyes now closed

like the pawnshop
across the street, its sign

blaring all night what
only daylight

can buy. Up
& down the block

you can hear the dogs talk—

never us—till the pigeons
pace the ledge

outside my bedroom & strut
like the painted girls down

on Twilight Avenue,
moan the morning blue.

THE SUIT

His fingers such a bad hand
of five-card

draw: trade
em all in & still

nothing. Same
crumby pair.

Thinking it was the wind
I let him, knocking, in

with a *shush* so's he wouldn't wake
the bruiser sleeping it off

in the other room. Half
of me hoped

to be caught, fought
over for once.
        No dice—

just that caller, no one's
gentleman, soaked

by rain or baptism

or bathtub gin—he sat
there in the dark that

dingied the room,
night a suit

of clothes, or cards,
he never quite fit.

Begged me like a bookie
for a second chance—

or least his money back.

Well bitten, his hands shook
in anticipation, thinking

this time at rummy he'll win—
discarding, declaring *Gin*.

Forgive me, then,
for reaching out

in the matchbook twilight—

strike here, close
cover before—

to better see him, to warm
his hands with mine & twine

together fingers one more time
before he went out

the way he came,
pockets still flat, all

bets off.
      Like drink,
there's never enough,

he thinks, of me around
in this dry

blue-law town.
In the growing light

I watched him like a house

on fire—helpless
to stop—going up

the hill,
　　　　he walked slow
as a man shouldering ice

he's cut himself
to sell, careful,

before it melts.

THE HEIST

Some tripped silent alarm

I empty round
after round as if at the bar

Hands trembling
like a suspension bridge

This bank heist gone
bad as a marriage.

Radio requesting backup

Me sweating bullets,
endless rounds

Outside, a sandwich board
hawking God

Shotgun smuggled
past security in a flower box

Black mask I can't see
squat out of.

Lady, let's slow drag
as the sirens sound closer

Well-paid police dog
on my tail—

Soon we'll be tropic, taking
baths in getaway green

Letting our skin ripen
& sweeten

The nights crisp
as a banknote Ben Franklin—

Put your hands
where we can see em

Hear the hounds
grow nearer, growl

Outside, the getaway car
leaking gas, tires shot

The megaphone hollering halt

My stethoscope cold
against the vault's locked heart

THE ESCAPE

My car, that dinosaur,
runs on memories

& other things older
than the fossil fuels I tell

the gas jockey to fill er
up with. I toss him

a few bits for his time
& hope he won't recognize me

& call the authorities—
whosoever they may be.

Before the dust
from my bald treads

settles, before he can wipe
the grease from his hands,

my skinny dime's ringing up
the solicitous sheriff

who rallies the posse.

My front-page face
lines every jailbird

& stool pigeon's cage.

I look dead
for my age—

or bout to be
if my shadow

ever catches up to me.

If they nab me I hope
like a catfish my whiskers

will spur their hands, turn
them numb

& like resignation I'll
give them the slip, swimming

into the dark, away.

More likely I'll end up
on someone's table

fileted & splayed.

Son, when you're drug
from the drink

they recognize you
by your tattoos—

I have none so I'll look
like everyone—

after all, a while,

we all smile
like a skull.

THE ALIBI

Searchlights gander
the city, I was convinced

looking for me. Convict
of nothing, believer

in the unsteady maps
of stars—I watched red-

nose regulars steam
themselves alive, downing

boilermakers by the bucket.

I tossed em back
myself like smallish fish

or dead soldiers—sent
out to sea, lit—lining

the corner table,
my usual.

Bartender opened me
like a church key

& I spilled everything—

her hair, her silent
offscreen kisses, all

but her real name

which everyone already knew
by number. Her legs long

like a gossip
column. Early

edition. The lobster shift.
Here at The Alibi

it's always late, and whenever
the phone rings

no one's in. It never

rings for me . . .
I see now that thinking

Joe over there's a regular
meant I was one too—that behind

the bar was a mirror
for a reason, not just

to make sure
it wadn't hunting season.

I'm tired of the city
telling me what it needs

isn't me—that mist is more
necessary to the picture

than I am. Pay
the man. Head outside

where the dark gathers round

fires built in the empty
barrel of the moon, men holding

their palms to its light
as if warmth. One hand

flint, the other
a stone—tonight I'll wander home

to sleep a few
hundred years & hope

her poison kiss might
slay me at last awake.

THE KILLER

Born on a showboat
headed upriver, he thought

the world a gamble
& the moon a gin-

soaked ice cube,
whole month

of melting. He looked a lot
like money, just not

much of it—thread-
bare, worn down

by use—stamped
by numbers & years,

a library book
long overdue. Heavy fines.

✳

You hated to find
yourself beneath

his oil-slick eyes—

the sweats would start
to overtake you

& you'd hitch a ride

on the potty train.
All aboard.

*

Wearing a splint
like a pinky ring,

he used a toothpick
like a cigarette—

collected guns
& grenades, their rings

long since yanked to take
someone's hand

like a bride.
Once he's been paid

you can't hide—
he'll find you & like

a jukebox fed a fistful
of change, plays his hits

without stopping,
maybe only to scratch.

*

      Crow's feet.

*

Have heard him called
a hundred things—

Sleep Stealer,
Death's Little Helper,

Dr. Dirt,
Mr. Red,

He-who-liketh-blood-
on-the-Outside-

Not-In,
The Professor,

The Bumpman,
St. Peter,

Jim Crow,
John Doe—

just never
late for dinner.

✳

No wonder
when he wandered

into Mojo Mike's—where I
was drinking whisky with a little

hot tea tossed in
to honey my throat—I thought

I was done. I skipped out

of there like a steak
done rare, wanting

no more blood
to spill from my side—

headed to the head
to hide.

✳

Widow's peak.

*

This is it,
I thought. So

long. Sayonara,
see ya,

no more, farewell,
friends, it's been swell—

ciao, air kiss,
adios amighost—

from now on my *nom
de plume*

is Toast.
Hereafter, hello.

*

Raven-haired.

*

He sat on down
& ordered—who knew

he ate at all, or liked the way
the food here was hot enough

to scar the roof
of your mouth & they let you

alone. The waitress could sense
whether you needed a menu

or carried one in your head
besides a to-do list:

Breathe, breathe,
patty melt, extra cheese.

Vinegar greens.

Through the bathroom door
that never quite closed,

while my stomach, half-
boiled, took a stab

at taps,
I watched him throw back

short ribs & anti-freeze,
drown his insides,

tip well & leave.

＊

From the bathroom, trying
not to breathe,

I thanked my stars
& knew if he had found me

like money
nothing could have saved me—

no gin, nor amen.

THE BALL

Like a suicide the band was
jumping, hitting high

then low, leaving
nothing but sweat

on the stand. I showed up
to the demimonde masquerade

disguised as myself

& no one recognized me.
My monkey suit still fit

better than I did—
I stuck out sideways

like my bow tie. In knots
over her quitting me,

I had to bogart
this 13th Annual

Bête Noire Ball—

Had some frail
on my arm (part

of my disguise), stars
shooting cross her eyes

from getting an invite—
but inside I was stag,

all solo. My eyes

watched my back
& the front door for

She-who-didn't-need-me

to enter. Incognito,
alleged, I waited

to get close or just
stare her from afar,

but that's, of course, par.

✳

On cue she enters,
her eyes 8-balls—dark

& darting & in the end
a prize. Behind them

is where I wanted to be.
At her side hung some guy

far wiser than me,

lipstick smearing
his cheek dark

as a bruise. She glides
the room like a dirigible

& I ain't able
to look away—burns

me up the way that gangster
orders her around

like a drink. Her twirled
pearls. Cloven shoes.

The police, paid off
by pastries, held up the walls

while all over the room
pomade waved like a beauty-pageant

winner right after.

✳

I had wanted to save her

like money, then hide
her away, a pearl

under an oyster's tongue.
That night, awkward,

cumberbound, I pretended
to chat like the rest

of the extras—moved uneasy
in the crowd as a mistress

at her man's funeral,
welcomed by no one,

yet known.

✳

Among these big fish
& wigs, among lobster bibs

& caviar thingamajigs

I felt like a crawdad
caught out of water, peeled

but quick. Puny me missed
them fish-sandwich women

back home who'd warm
your side & only wanted

some time, a little talk.
Here every painting hides

a million bucks, or none—deeds
locked in a safe—& the ladies'

fingers have enough rocks
to start a garden, a quarry

no chain gang could break.

✳

Even in this
thief's paradise there was little

I wanted: her
smooth hands in mine

dancing slow for a time.
The rest was preface.

After taking a whole roll

of film with my boutonniere,
I had downed enough courage

to cross the room & brush by her
like a pickpocket, stealing

a glance that telegraphed
Meet me in 5.

She did, for old times,
or one last—

As my misplaced date
hovered by the food

& ate with her hands
& eyes, we snuck out

by the pool. I wonder

if it, too, was pulled
by the moon.

✳

Around us, frost.

She shivered in her
X-ray dress

so I gave her my jacket,
price tag still in it.

Over time we'd learned
to skip the weather

& *howdy* & the *how-
could-yous*—

To forego the fight entirely

& head, like the heavyweight
finally defeated, to the silence

& bruise & antiseptic
of after. There,

while shadows gathered
in the deep end

I could not swim,

we kissed & my bow tie
turned a whirligig, lifted

me high among the trees
till I could see

how far I'd fall, that between us
air was all

we had left. My eyes oysters

pried open—
shucks.

Her pearlies
a piano I almost forgot

how to play, never got
practice enough.

*

Didn't want

to let go her hand & sink
back into the blue

but knew I had to. No more

could we disappear
into the dark like a tooth

left in a glass
of cola, or the moon

that, even unseen,
still tugged at us,

sick dentist. Still
we danced awhile

at the lip of the pool, slow
dragging like a cigar

*

till she stole like thunder
back inside

to her life of smiling
when he said to, of betting

against her own chances.
I counted *Mississippis*

to make sure I didn't follow
too close or brave

lightning twice,
then headed inside

where the party began
breaking things

& up—the drummer taking
down his trap, the bass again

silent, the saxophonist splitting
apart his horn

shaped like a question mark.
We are all

built to be done, remarked
no one.

After confetti, we'll sweep on

home separately
to sleep like enemies:

lightly, dreaming only
of each other's loaded arms.

MIDNIGHT RAMBLE

Leaving the coffin-cold
theater in winter

Single-barrel moon
aimed above us

He escorted & told me
lies I wanted

To warm my ears

The moon's lazy eye
razored shut

The two of us
fought that hawk

Walking through wind
across a world that once

Seemed so flat I feared
I might could fall off—

*Now, Clare, every horizon
got another behind it*

Least that's what
Mama would say—*Just you wait*—

But I hightailed it north
& changed my name.

Beneath the shrapnel sky
I wanted to run

From here to the train
& buy me a ticket one way—

I'm tired of eviction
The radio's same station

Playing woe & blues

Said tired of eviction
The radio's same station

Arguing whose man is whose.

I want some diesel bound
south, making all stops—

No more neighbor's
whooping cough

No more leaky
solos from the faucets

Or landlords who pinch,
swapping winks for late rent.

Graveyard-shift moon
that turns men mad—

Let me trade fire
escape for front porch

Let me ride
sunset down to where

Train's the only whistle

& a girl don't got to cry
to keep herself company

Where moonshine ain't just sky
& you can catch catfish

Sure as a man—bearded, polite—
already fixed up & fried.

THE DIVE

Young men here guzzle
& dream of becoming drunks

& regulars, the drunks
here dream of becoming

young. I wait

for her one hour, promise
myself no more, then wait

half hour over.
As I'm pretending

to don my fedora, some hood

arrives to tell me she ain't
coming, never, no matter

& I better quit callin.
Pats his pistol-padded side.

I wish that I was a wish,

that rubbing this bottle—
gin's djinni—would give me

more than mist.
The stooge suggests

I find another date,

to learn a place
where the smoke don't stain you

& the glasses wash up new.
Like fatback

his knuckles crack.

I excuse myself to the head,
looking for an escape hatch—

cursing her name, planning
never to forget her.

She gets under

& infiltrates, she's foreign
intelligence . . .

No dice. Windows sealed
by the past & paint—

Dreaming of a back way

I read some last words
on the wall, faint—

*Don't sleep
With a gangster*

Or his wife. Just don't.

Nor a waitress,
some wise guy retorts.

Then something I don't
remember penning—

Reports of my death are

greatly anticipated—
but it's my hand sure

as shooting.

THE PAYBACK

Stripped, de-
briefed,

cowed, found
out, frisked,

confessed, pled,

tired, treed,
left for dead

& for good, forgot—

lurched, lost,
scalded, belted, shook,

rooked, finked, ratted
out & on—

withdrawn, strapped,

harried, pursued, deluded,
deluged—

bit by dogs
hounding my heels—

jilted, jinxed,

downed, fawned
over, ferreted,

sated & abetted, sent

into the lion's
living room—

parlayed, parlor-
tricked, sicced

on, surrendered—
quailed, quitted, shown

the door, the boot, given

the bum's rush,
the lady's luck—

botched, black-
listed, decked, sawed

in half, duped,

dried out, dusted
off, sobered, handed

my hat, running out
of excuses & room—

I came clean.
Forgive me.

As in the dream when you turn
to face them that chase you

up the endless stairs
I spun

& found no one.

Turns out all
that hunted me

was me—haunted
by what I believed

she to be. So I gave up
some green, flashed

a few fins around town,
greased

the underworld's
squeaky wheels

& got let off free. Left
to my own devices—

which are few,
& idiot-proof.

She was permanent yet
faded, a prison

tattoo—I once thought
like that serum

she'd be true

but I know now
I was wrong as a sweater

on a sheepdog.

SOUNDTRACK

Banging out a symphony
in a typewriter key, I didn't hear

My door creak open, only
her *Ah-hum* & perfume

My knocking knees

When, uninvited, she sat
herself down. Crossed

Her legs like the county line

& I, some boot-
legger driven far

For such strong lightning.

She leaned & asked
once more could I find—

A friend? her man?
something so valuable

She could not say?

Anythin,
was once my answer—

Had spent off-meter hours,
hundreds, snooping for her

Working under the cover—

Was left with only
a fake-mustache rash

& some prop glasses
without glass.

My heart twin
cufflinks then.

*

Tonight, her eyes welling
over like an oil rig,

I let my mind, like
a housewife, or eye, wander:

August again
    & I eleven, filled with Sunday

& early supper—
    hummocked, happy.

How the sycamores sang,
    the cicadas.

This is long before
    gunfire, before the Colt

& rope & a river
    I am still swimming.

Long before I arrived
    our starved city, before derringer days

& nights even darker for all
    the streetlights . . .

Her hands tapped
an impatient Morse, fanned

Two lace gloves. *Well?*
Her veil smile.

Adam's-apple bob. Ceiling-fan swirl.

✳

I thanked her for
her time, then sent her

Away packing, teetering
on unsheathed stilettos.

Her kisses tender, a resignation—

I may be back
to her like an undertaker

Whose scent no one can shake—

For now I'll ignore the lack
of knocking, the quiet

Except for wind
& tin-roof rain,

The phone's pleading ring.

CREDITS

The city at last let me
leave it—streetlights

just on—no sunset—
the scent

of laundry rising up
from beneath a grate,

starched by hands
unseen—Mama's,

I imagine. I have had
it all, enough

of water cold & clogged—

have a mind, half,
to walk these weedy blocks

to the station where a midnight

train tugged me
nine months back. I step

careful, avoiding the cracks.

Everywhere,
late-summer hum—

no crickets, just the smack
& holler of children playing

stickball—no
mound, no sliding,

no nothing but beans
& pork, asphalt & fence, far

as I can see. Stoop talk.

You can keep your cans,
kick em all day—

I can taste already
Mama's tomatoes coming up

from the earth like a mummy
—slow, heavy, hungry—

in the B movie I always
end up in, playing

Screaming Girl, Secretary,
or Victim #2. I always did feel

sorry for that man wrapped up
in his past, made awake

by grave robbers as if newlywed
neighbors. *How d'you do?*

The name's Clarice—
though down home everyone knows

to call me Reece & not
to bother phoning, just

drop on by. The train lurches
the station—all points south—

till I am a star like all the others
in sky—winking, flashing strings

of pearls like citified words—
flickering like the Luckies

I will hide, buried
with pride & *told you so*s

beneath our unscreened porch.

FIN

from

FOR THE CONFEDERATE DEAD

{ **2007** }

This is a beautiful country.

{ JOHN BROWN }
on his way to the gallows

ELEGY FOR MISS BROOKS

i.m. Gwendolyn Brooks 1917–2000

There's nothing left
to say. You have done
      your dance, away—
to the place we never thought
  would gather you

though somewhere we knew
how days grow shorn. Unbrittle,
      brave, graceful yet laceless,
you struck the stone till you were
  the stone, or the face

each dark rock hides, if only
from itself. Somethin else. The water
      wears over us—
headed home, salt-ward.
  We wade in your wake

& pray. Forever
bendable, you never did stoop—
      whenever sidewalk's hard heat
met your dandelion wild,
  you fought that white

head through.
A thankful while, the wind
      our way blew.
Without you, we might not know
  what wind must do—

it too refuses to remain
unseen, keeps many names.
      Gust, bluster, hurricane,
Bronzeville's heavy hawk—
  you swirl & save us

from standing still,
unsailed. What the devil
      are we without you?
I tuck your voice, laced
   tight, in these brown shoes.

THE BALLAD OF JIM CROW

*from the life
& lore of The Killer
a.k.a.
Mister Red, Doctor Death,
Professor Limbo, John Doe
& Jim Crow*

NATIVITY

Known by four score
& seven names, Jim Crow
was born
with a silver bullet

in his hand. Some say
on a gambling boat,
others say he met the world
at home, in a shotgun

shack. For certain
his left hand clutched
a tin nickel
swallowed by his mother

so the taxman
couldn't touch it.
That boy was all
she had.

The day was grey.
The night dark brown.
A twister was spotted
all over town.

Jim's middle name
was None.
His first left blank
for a few hours

till Mr. Crow came home
& called for *Gin*.
No cigars. Birth certificate
an afterthought—

back there then the county
only thought about you
when you were dead.
Or born silver—

unlike Jim, this wooden
spoon in his mouth
the midwife promptly took
& spanked him awake with.

Welcome.

TRINITY

Jim Crow's first cousin was Rust.

His reddish head followed
Jim everywhere,
turning into his name
everything Rust touched.

Jim's sister was nicknamed Sleep.
Everyone wanted to meet
her, or meet more
of her. She was known to snore

to wake the dead, which
is what Everyone would be if
Jim ever caught on.
On the front porch he shone

his gun like the sun.
For any suitor fool enough
to ask after Sleep
Jim promised a dirt nap

& that's just a start.
Out back he had begun to plant
row after row
of empty graves like cotton holes

waiting to be sown.

TEMPTATION

Jim Crow and Rust loved
to pick fights. Hated
picking cotton. Dug
the ladies, though beauty

mostly puzzled the pair, those
few who bothered to notice
the duo's dusty clothes,
their accents thick as country mice.

Rust had a way with machines.
Could make the broken sing
& when he had him a few drinks
did just that. His favorite

sport was thirst,
which only made things worse.
Stuffed on air sandwiches,
hard as tomorrow's bread

& as broke, they'd wander roads
hoping for more. They picked
fights with The Devil
or each other in order

not to have to fight
someone bigger. To impress.
Folks began calling Jim
Killer, and Rust

Rust. Around thin necks
they stuck out only
for each other, they'd cinch
& loosen like a noose the one tie

they shared, never did lose.

TABERNACLE

Since they shared the same
monogram, Jim
Crow & Jesus
often found themselves

getting the other's dress shirts
back from the wash.
This was after Jim
had made it big

& could afford such
small luxuries. He
& Jesus mostly met
Sundays in church

where Jesus came for the singing
but stayed for the sermon
& to see whether the preacher
ever got it right.

Jim, you guessed it,
came for the collection plate
& after stayed
for the hot

plates of the Ladies
Auxiliary (no apostrophe).
To one
folks prayed,

the other they obeyed.

BAPTISM

Jim's duel with The Devil

was quick as Hell.
The Devil won,
of course, always does,
but afterward taught Jim a trick

or two. How to keep things close
to the vest, to dress
& impress, how to play
dumb, or numb, to play

cards & keeps.
The Devil lived on Such
& Such Street, kept
an office at the crossroads

by a gnarled tree.
SOULS FOR SALE his sign
read in red. His smile
was beautiful—mostly

a partial from a dentist
just outside Houston, near Hell's
third circle. Poor Jim
loved little—his cousin

Rust, sister Sleep
who he watched over
& even prayed for—
Jim felt like an orphan

& meant to make
the world feel it too.
To know his name.
There, There

said The Devil, who hides
a soft side, despite
what they say.
Have a drink on me

pull up a chair
& bend my pointy ear.
Then poured a tall
glass of lye

for bruised Jim to eye.

ASCENSION

The sun set
on all his arguments.
At midnight roosters
called out

his name.
Jim Crow crowed
not at all.
The sun set

in its ways.
Heart in a sling.
Jim's neck in a brace
like a bow tie

for his court case.
For insurance sake.
Always on trial,
Jim was—

the State defended
Jim Crow to the death
& always won. Jim had him
a huge green file.

Jim slept with one
eye open,
hand clenching
his daddy's gun.

The sun just set
there like a lazy dog.
The sinking ship
of the eclipse. Jim

spitshining the silver
bullet he was born with.

✳

Jim's fingerprints
always found
at the scene—sheriffs
must've carried them

in their belts besides
their billy clubs & star-
shaped badges.
Jim's song was a smack

in the skull—
a dark drum.
The discipline
of a nun.

Only at night did Jim Crow soar
where the Big
Dipper's drinking gourd
dared pour.

From jail Jim's escape
would take a dozen
dark days.
Took one deputy

paid off
to look the other way
& a birthday cake
with a file for filling

Sleep had gone & baked.

*

One day Jim
just up
& flew away.
One day.

After his daring escape
Jim Crow's name would soon
be fame.
Posted all over town

at lunch counters
& water fountains.
Like a sun
Jim shone

his gun.
Alone,
all over town,
the sun set

like a broken bone.

DESCENT

Assassins sleep
like babies, deep
& fitful, it's the rest
of us who pace

& pace, undreaming.
Or dreaming what
we haven't done.
Easier to forget

than regret—
Jim knew this,
slept easy
as the money he made

taking out the faithless,
or knocking off
those who thought
for a moment fate

wasn't watching.
Who tried to siphon off
a bit of the bounty,
or sleep with beauty

as if that could last.
It wasn't the cash
Jim Crow was after,
but to put right

what couldn't be,
or hadn't ever been.
His victims
were lucky, patients

really & he
Doctor Red
helping them along.
Their eyes coins already.

Least they went
quick, had a choice—
unlike Rust
who bit it slow

& steady & fading
as his name

Jim dared not dream.

MAGNIFICAT

Now that he was rich
Jim Crow didn't
act like it—done
with sharkskin suits

& linen, he learned
to patch his clothes
& count every coin
like a sin. His woolens

worn away like a record
played too much,
the houndstooth warped
like Bessie's broad voice.

Each month he sent
his mother a bundle
though the two
rarely spoke. Enclosed

is a little something
for food, he wrote.
And when Rust went
wherever the dead did

Jim sprung for all
expenses, ordered the best casket
at Bloodworth's Funeral Home.
The dam of his eyes broke

& Jim couldn't go.
Each Sunday
Jim's mother gave over
her take to God

who didn't ask where
the bread came from.
Neither did she.
Still, every once in a moon

his mother bought
herself a church hat
with shoes to match—
not to hide

her face, but frame
its blossom brown
& remind folks
that humility

need not be ugly.
Beneath her hat, its bright
unfading flowers,
Jim's mother lowers

her head & prays.
For her son's soul. For Sleep
to return. For freedom
from this toil

& the red red soil.
It's me,
Lord, Jim's mama said,
bent her hatted head

& clenched like teeth
her hands.
It's me Lord,
she reminded

herself, whose mother
named her America
and whose father was born
a slave

but died free—
which is better
than the other
way round, if you ask me.

GUERNICA

Survivors will be human.
—MICHAEL S. HARPER

It's all there in black
and white: someone
has done it again.

We have lynched a man

in a land far-off
like Texas, hog-tied
and -wild

to the back of a car.

There's a word I have been
searching for
in the sand but cannot find.

✳

At five o'clock in the afternoon

we play ball, hard,
in Spanish
until we bruise

No trash
talk, no beautiful
rejections—just these

shots, the smooth
skull of the ball
and that

slant Andalusian light

*

Nearby they are burying
the boy beaten
by the gang—nobody

knows him, everyone

calls the killers by name.
Names. With handcuffs some
manage to hide

their faces like furnaces

failing—first flame, then smoke
and now only cold.

*

It shifts, this light,
its bruised eye shines

above our heads.
Before us the horse,
javelin-tongued, about

to whinny a word—
that wildness in the eyes.
Again, the bull

horning in—how many
has he drug
silent into swamp

or South, whether of States
or Spain?
If it moans

like a man it must
be a man.

＊

One day the writer
the painter rose

excused himself from the table
at which he no longer

could sit still.
Still sit.

Bought him a one-way
billet, boarded the train

or the boat bound
for Paris

land of red and blue

＊

Dragged awake by midday
light, hunger
sweating my sheets.

We go out into heat. Sit
shaded and peel the shrimp
we will eat, and laugh.

Seafood fresh as a wound.

＊

Precious South,
must I save you

or myself?
On the day of the saint

we watch from the terrace
trying not to toss

ourselves over like flowers.
In the arena

the bulls bow, and begin.
Above the roar the victor

will save
the ear, the living leather.

PRAYER

Today even the cows are tired
have lain down, tuckered, tucking
their legs beneath them

in prayer. Their thick restless
tongues, tails, their blank
bovine bows.

No wonder we worship cows.

No wonder we let them lick
the salt from our arms.
Or bend beneath them

& borrow their motherhood
make it our own. Have you ever
tasted fresh-pulled milk, slightly

warm? It tastes of whatever
grass you have fed them: blue
or bitter crab. Mint. No wonder

we swallow cows & save
their skins, find out if we fit.

AMERICANA

It occurs to me that I am America.
I am talking to myself again.
—ALLEN GINSBERG

America, you won't obey.
You won't hunt
or heel or stay.

America, you won't do
anything I want you to.
(To tell the truth,
I like that about you.)

You're too much.

What mountains you are
America! What minefields
and mysteries, symptoms
and cinemas and symphonies
and cemeteries!

Bully, albino, my
   lopsided love—

America, I can't leave you
well enough alone.

America, you've lost
your way home—

I have saluted
your dying woods, called to
   your flags trimmed on tin.

America, I am letting you in.
America, where you been?

I have seen your tiny twilit eyes
   your mouth still
   stuffed with straw.
I have driven your bent unbroken
   back and fallen
   to my knees like a nun

   in her black habit
praying you would change.

Today the road runs straight

Today the grey
is yours! the fog
and the burning leaves.

Today the crows refuse
to get out the way

Today I drive the rains
of your rough face
   your citified plains—

America, won't you take
   your hands of hurt away?
   tuck them drawer-deep
   like the good
   silver of grandmothers?

(I have inherited, America, only
   rusty knees, a voice
hoarse from hollering.)

America I have counted
   all the china and none
   is missing.

America, I love most your rust,
    the signs that misspell doom—

And why not your yards
    of bottle trees and cars?

And why not the heart
    transplants we want?

America, tell the maples
    to quit all this leaving.

Warranty up, trial basis,
    thirty days free—

America I have seen
    men whose faces are flags
    bloodied and blue with talk

seen the churches keep
    like crosses burning

seen the lady who lines
    your huddled shore, her hand
    rifle-raised,
    her back turned away.

THRONE OF THE THIRD HEAVEN OF THE NATIONS MILLENNIUM GENERAL ASSEMBLY

James Hampton, self-taught artist

Evenings I return with my head
Soaked with stars—place
A crown crafted of foil
On my head and set to work

By day I sweep the school
Nights I piece together heaven
The way God intended:
By hand, by saving
What some would throw away

No one sees scraps are what saves

What do I know of purgatory?
Except the cans that once a week
Congregate along the curb, waiting
To be delivered

Some of what I need I find
Among those rusty lids, past peels
And maggots
The metal gleaming

What we gather, we are

When I die and make
My way to that third place
The land-
Lord will discover this

Altar above my garage
Decide it art
Find the faith my hands wound
Each day like a watch
My magpiety

FOR THE CONFEDERATE DEAD

I go with the team also.
—WHITMAN

These are the last days
my television says. Tornadoes, more
rain, overcast, a chance

of sun but I do not
trust weathermen,
never have. In my fridge only

the milk makes sense—
expires. No one, much less
my parents, can tell me why

my middle name is Lowell,
and from my table
across from the Confederate

Monument to the dead (that pale
finger bone) a plaque
declares war—not Civil,

or Between
the States, but for Southern
Independence. In this café, below sea-

and eye-level a mural runs
the wall, flaking, a plantation
scene most do not see—

it's too much
around the knees, height
of a child. In its fields Negroes bend

to pick the endless white.
In livery a few drive carriages
like slaves, whipping the horses, faces

blank and peeling. The old hotel
lobby this once was no longer
welcomes guests—maroon ledger,

bellboys gone but
for this. Like an inheritance
the owner found it

stripping hundred years
(at least) of paint
and plaster. More leaves each day.

In my movie there are no
horses, no heroes,
only draftees fleeing

into the pines, some few
who survive, gravely
wounded, lying

burrowed beneath the dead—
silent until the enemy
bayonets what is believed

to be the last
of the breathing. It is getting later.
We prepare

for wars no longer
there. The weather
inevitable, unusual—

more this time of year
than anyone ever seed. The earth
shudders, the air—

if I did not know
better, I would think
we were living all along

a fault. How late
it has gotten . . .
Forget the weatherman

whose maps move, blink,
but stay crossed
with lines none has seen. Race

instead against the almost
rain, digging beside the monument
(that giant anchor)

till we strike
water, sweat
fighting the sleepwalking air.

GUINEA GALL

And one day, when, I will cross
Great Water, walk and reach
that final rise

to find them
singing. There,
in the valley, they all will be.

Forgive me, Grandfather, for wanting
to hear you again
for leaning close to strain

to understand what you are saying.
And Mother, Father, for expecting
to kiss again your wide hands

even though I still can.
In my breast
pocket I shall keep

the ticket the conductor
sold me
stamped One Way.

That day even rain can't delay.

And we will sit and rock
and sip our sweating drinks—
watching the sun toward us bring

red light like an arriving train.

APRIL IN PARIS

Lionel Hampton's Last Weekend in Concert at the
Hotel Meridien, Paris, Good Friday, 1999

The light dim
as they bring him—
    Ladies & Gentleman
Mademoiselles & Monsieurs

    Lionel Hampton!—in—
His cane quick turns
    to a xylophone wand—
Dad says the man used to hold

    two at a time—strikes
notes clear as a river
    or its gold.
Motherlode. He's slowed

    some, plenty—
like M'Dear, 102, who
    one night fell off
the porch she thought

    a bathroom, then lay till dawn
leg broken—her last
    and his. (Still, sometimes
you gotta make a break

    for it, like the time
they found M'Dear, eleven then,
    along the highway
with baby brother

having decided to walk
back to their old, all-black home
in Bouley, Oklahoma
where a sign in town proclaimed

WHITES NOT ALLOWED
PAST SUNDOWN.)
Playing the subtleties
of silence, Hampton traces,
like a government agency,

the vibes—quietly—
his wands a magic,
a makeshift. Arthritic solos

hover like a bee
above the flower, finding
the sweet center.
Two days before Easter, Monsieur

Hampton plays the changes,
offering up
songs read off
a napkin bruised with lyrics:

*What did I do
to be so black & blue?*
his voice wobbles
along the highway

called history,
flying home. Here.
(Leaves out the part
I'm white—inside—

because he's not.)
The band, tight, will swarm
            behind & save him
if he falls—when—

            The sax player stops
between tunes to dab
            a handkerchief at the drool
gathering his chin.

            Such
care. The mind's blind
            alleys we wander down.
This is enough, just—

            This is Paris—

In the Rosa Parks section,
            as the drummer we met
before the second set
            dubbed it, we stand

            in the back
& applaud
            & shout *yeah*
& block no one.

            And I say to myself
What a wonderful world—

            Dad's so excited
he falls off
            the risers—& he laughs
& we laugh—

Skies are blue
Clouds are white

Sacred dark light

In which, after, they lead him out.

POSTSCRIPTS

The world is a widow.

Storms surround us, areas
of low

& high pressure
moving through—

should be gone tomorrow.

Rain from the sky
like planes.

We pull ourselves up
from bed
or death, wander

streets like ghosts,
lost guests.
Everyone's a town

with the shops shutting
down, no hours
posted. Even the radio

stays closed—only news
or fools still

believing love.
Traffic that won't move.

In the crossing, a white hearse
hanging a left.

I want to be that woman
just ahead, tapping her foot
out a car window, bare,

in time to a music
I can't quite hear.

SEPTEMBER 2001

AFRICAN ELEGY
(MUCH THINGS TO SAY)

i.m. Philippe Wamba, 1971–2002

•

One good thing about music
When it hits you feel no pain

{ BOB MARLEY }

THE NEWS [STOP THAT TRAIN]

When you died I was reading Whitman
   aloud.
While you died I was miles away,
     thousands of deserts and oceans
     and mountains and plain.
When you went I was reading aloud the end
     to a crowd trying
     to remember how grief once felt,
     wanting to forget,
     wanting not to.
While you went about that dangerous road
     on your way was it to the sea
I was saying *Look for me*
     under your bootsoles.
Caked with mud.
Caked with mud the color
     of blood, the picture much
     later I saw of your truck
     totaled, towed
     by what was left
     of the axles—
Your passenger brother's breath a miracle.
When you died I was reading aloud
     for the dead, for what
     I had almost believed
     and then the world went
And did this. I cannot forgive
     this world, its gear's unsteady turn,
     that day's sun that shone
While you died trying to get home.

11 SEPTEMBER 2002

It is late when we decide
   the long flight to you, to find
   repellent enough to keep
   even this away.
It is late when I think I cannot make it
   and am afraid—
   I can't, my passport
   is old, the picture
   I took to tour Europe
   with you barely looks
   like me now, and yours
   I can no more remember.
It is early when I go
   get the shots to keep
   me well—you understand
   they give you a little
   now to let it
   later not kill you.
There's no immunity
   against grief—
There's nothing that keeps
   away dengue fever
   or a hundred other
   harms—
Boil or tablet the water.
Another pill to take
   the taste out.
Are you ok without meningitis?
I am ok I think I leave
   then go back and get more
   to make my arm sore.
This one lasts you
   for life
This one lasts four months

This one take
   every day while there
   and seven days after.
This one you don't need
This one won't take effect
   till you return.

Perhaps grief itself
   is inoculation against
   it all, faith
   is much of it—
I half forget
   and hug myself
   and there it is again—
   the pain—
For you my arms ache for days.

17 SEPTEMBER

THE FUNERAL ROAD [BABYLON BY BUS]

Honey's Fashions
on road to the family home

white mannequins
in the window
selling something I can't see

*

last night when we landed
in Dar es Salaam the smell everywhere
of fireworks in the air

as if something nearby exploded

and no one in the road

*

Que's Cyber Café on the way
to funeral

right side of his face/fallen

hearse a small bus with a siren

I'll follow him
forever

*

dozens of blondwood beds
frames empty

Asante Yehova
on a billboard

Thank You Jehovah
For Answering Our Prayers

✳

a rooster walking
under a vanity
its oblong mirror

✳

Survey Motel
self contained rooms

photocopy binding

✳

red dirt in a pile
high enough
for a hundred graves

✳

Relatives & Freinds
misspelled on our bus

✳

along the long
road to the chapel
one boy saluting

another aiming
his elbow at us
and shooting

20 SEPTEMBER

BURIAL [NO WOMAN NO CRY]

We circle the grave
in dark coats like buzzards.
The men, me too, this morning
had lifted you, steering

your wooden ship through
metal doors to the living room.
I couldn't stand to see
the screws still loose.

A plank it felt we walked.
They lifted the lid
right there and we filed
past like ants, bearing

twice our weight
in sorrow. It wasn't
true. That ain't you—
too grey, and serious,

right side of your face
fallen, cotton
filling your nose—
at least the suit looked new.

We held each other a long time
after and could not speak,
like you. Get up,
Stand up, we'll sing

later, the reggae you loved
your brother will strum
stumbling on a guitar, and for
a moment you'll be there, here,

where we'd been brought to visit
too late, like fools.
At the grave we step
past crumbling stones

and dead flowers to stand
on the red rise
of dirt already dug
for you. The sound

of them letting you down.
The sound of men scraping
and scraping what
I can't quite see, spreading

the cool concrete
over you by hand. And it takes
long, so long, like death—
like we once thought life.

The choir lifts us up
with their voices above
the coconut trees—*Habari
Jemba* they sing—

and the tune tells me Isn't That
Good News.
Cell phones chiming
their songs too.

After, we place white flowers
on your hardening tomb.
Is it only the sun
we shade our faces from?

Our sweat a thousand tears.

21 SEPTEMBER

SABBATH [WAIT IN VAIN]

And all Sunday we slept

starting once
and then again
asleep, wake

only when it's dark.
It's one
in the night

Swahili time—
we've learned now
to wear our watches

upside down.
We want to see
your town—that you there

on the corner,
haggling
with God?

Later we'll sneak
& chew *tchat* in honor
of you, keeping you

hidden in our cheeks
for hours. You are
the Tusker

downed warm,
the chili sauce we sweat
our kingfish with,

fruit we don't dare touch.
Scrabble your fiancée's mother
always wins.

HOMESIT. HONEY-
ED. I want
to stay here

forever, or for you,
to see how happy
your life might

make me, us
left to live it
for you.

And tomorrow
back to the work
that is life, grief, what's

left: climbing
the church tower
till we can't go

any higher, creaking up
the spire past the bells
I want to ring

but it's too early.
Down again, we'll wait
in the churchyard & watch

children playing tag, taunting
whoever's it & pretending
safe. Walk on

down to a jetty
where men line up pissing
into the unmoved sea,

the shore rocking
a tide full of bottles
like wishes washed

back empty.

STONE TOWN [HIGH TIDE OR LOW TIDE]

We decide the last

minute, day we are
   to leave, to fly for a tour

of Zanzibar—
   the prop plane pulling far

above the city and shore
   that you loved, leaving

the ground like bodies behind.
   Shadows of clouds

across green water.
   Whatever I fear,

a fall, does not happen, or has
   happened already—who can

say. You're gone.
   And the sun

pays no mind, still leaves
   the water blues and green

and colors I cannot name
   but imagine you always

had a word for. Stone Town
   itself is beautiful and loud

and lush, fish split open
   like mouths in the market, cats

waiting for what falls.
    The Joba Tree, tall—

where slaves once were tied and sold
    and whipped to show

how strong—
    long since chopped down.

Red marble
    in the chapel

built over the stump.
    Here, the House of Wonder

is mostly empty, a few rusty
    Communist cars—and at last we reach

ocean bare feet can feel,
    fruit you can peel

and trust. Nose full of dust.
    Today's never enough—

the flight back too quick
    while the pilot barely looks,

fills out forms and carbons.
    In sunset Dar es Salaam

spread out against the ocean
    like a hand.

You're gone.
    Below, drifting plumes

of smoke. Can it be
    too much to hope—

that tonight the sailboats
　　will fill their wings

with wind and skim
　　home quickly

across the sky of sea.

CATCH A FIRE

I arrive home to cyclones,
to trees broken like the heat
hasn't yet. Autumn
nowhere in sight except

a few leaves starting
their fall fire. Driving without
eyes for wreckage,
I don't notice right away—

Otis Redding sings A Change
Is Gonna Come and I sob
one last time you're gone.
High up, the BILLIONS

SOLD sign mangled,
once golden arches turned
almost an ampersand—
a few miles along it dawns

what storms I've missed.
Signs ripped down.
Roofs made only of tarp.
Pink tongues of insulation

pulled from the mouths
of houses now silent.
*Looking for a sign
from God?*

one billboard asks—
This is it.
What's left
of the Hillview Motel

no longer needs say
VACANCY.
Only the hill
still here. The corn

brown and shorn.
In a few weeks who can tell
what's being built
and what torn down—

flattened, the fields
all look the same. For now
this charcoal smell
fluttering past the hill—

It's been too hard living

And I'm afraid to die—
the thick smoke billowing
from burning
what's still green

but can't be saved.

25 SEPTEMBER

REDEMPTION SONG

Finally fall.
At last the mist,
heat's haze, we woke
these past weeks with

has lifted. We find
ourselves chill, a briskness
we hug ourselves in.
Frost greying the ground.

Grief might be easy
if there wasn't still
such beauty—would be far
simpler if the silver

maple didn't thrust
its leaves into flame,
trusting that spring
will find it again.

All this might be easier if
there wasn't a song
still lifting us above it,
if wind didn't trouble

my mind like water.
I half expect to see you
fill the autumn air
like breath—

At night I sleep
on clenched fists.
Days I'm like the child
who on the playground

falls, crying
not so much from pain
as surprise.
I'm tired of tide

taking you away,
then back again—
what's worse, the forgetting
or the thing

you can't forget.
Neither yet—
last summer's
choir of crickets

grown quiet.

19 OCTOBER

EULOGY [PEOPLE GET READY]

And so the snow.

Far away the cactus flowering.

White morning making

my hands sting.

Lilies in a refrigerator

losing scent.

Tell me the weather

wherever you are.

Let snow send its angels—

lay down and wave

numb arms.

Deepening drifts.

We who are left

like mailboxes along a country road

huddle together in the cold

awaiting word.

5 DECEMBER

ONE LOVE

Long ladder
    the rain makes

The thirsty
    throat of God—

The night of the day
we buried you
we sang every
Bob Marley song we knew

by heart or whatever
it was that kept
us up, and together—
call it *gut*—

It sure wasn't
legs that kept anyone
that day moving
numb.

A fork
    in the road like a tongue

Long night
    the heat makes—

The wide open mouth
of your brother's guitar
Your mother & us making music
to shut the silence

that is nowhere
but where
you might be, planted
beneath the palm trees.

We sway
        how long I cannot say

Long ladder
        of wished-for rain—

Later that night
we each sing some
song that is ours,
whatever we know—by gut—

& I sing the thing
that's kept me
company all day:
It's me It's me

It's me O Lord
        standing in the need

Of prayer—
        It's me It's me It's me—

O Lord—

Your fiancée tall
& sleepless
One brother strumming
One outside smoking

And another already
quiet under a hill.
The old song
my love sang:

From this valley they say
  you are going

We will miss your bright
  eyes & sweet smile—

Later your father
giving stories to the dawn
tells of his great-uncle
who lived to be

one hundred
twenty-two years old
& was still
going strong—

Know how he died?
  He took his own life

Left a note saying *God*
  has forgotten me.

It's me It's me
O Lord—
Tonight I
and I are afraid

we may have slipped
God's mind—
Above us
the stubbed-out stars

The dark unmoving
       mouth of the guitar—

Tonight, by gut,
I pray you are
God—
but not forgotten—

O earth
       of a thousand exits

O endless
endings—
Why does waiting
feel like pain

& pain waiting?
How to finish
this song,
say my goodbye—

Long ladder
       the days make

Short time
       to climb.

SPRING 2003

COMMENCEMENT

Already the apartments
unfilling. Steady rain.
The feeling of rented

gowns against the skin.
Of rented everything.
That rain

again. The green—
loud sound of digging,
whine from a far-off machine.

Tornadoes take away
whole towns,
touching down. Families

try to find
each other, pointing out
their child in the crowd—

That one's mine,
proud. Teams practice
sliding home

dusting off uniforms
& somewhere the tailor is bored
to tears with nothing

left to hem. Rained
out games—
But the flowers love it

says the man selling me
sweet tea.
In my yard what I thought

were only weeds
turns out are really
a hundred tiny

blooming maple trees.

HOMAGE TO PHILLIS WHEATLEY

{ 1998–2011 }

Phillis was brought from *Africa* to *America* in the Year 1761, between Seven and Eight Years of Age. Without any Assistance from School Education, and by only what she was taught in the Family, she, in sixteen Months Time from her Arrival, attained the English Language, to which she was an utter Stranger before, to such a Degree, as to read any, the most difficult Parts of the Sacred Writings, to the great Astonishment of all who heard her.

{ JOHN WHEATLEY }

Religion indeed has produced a Phyllis Whately; but it could not produce a poet.

{ THOMAS JEFFERSON }
Notes on the State of Virginia

ON BEING BROUGHT
FROM AFRICA TO AMERICA

At your back dusk.
At your back stars
and this abiding sense
of what you would since

call *God*. The auction
block, the boat that rocked
and renamed you *Phillis*—
your young back the driver's lash

(maybe) managed not to meet.
The writer's toil, and prayer,
promising you immortal—
this foreign, frosted soil.

Latinate black girl, what
the Lord leaves us is this:—
your mother's voice pressed
fainter each day; thick dust.

ON IMAGINATION

First poet of your Race,
you could be nothing but servant
in these States—learning Rs
to say *The Lord*, not learning *you*
but *Thou*. How thy face

lit up among the oil lamps each week
you had to clean! Sable
sister—at least your master
did not make you with him
(we think) sleep, or

out in the stable. Your world was now
whispers and *Sincerelys*—on the block
Master Wheatley bought you off,
you must have thought (though most thought
you could not):—Such strange beasts

haggling over me! My head must
stay covered, my must must
not show. I shall be the girl's
plaything, taking orders, learning
to write in order to tell

what I am not. Thankful,
yes, I am for that:—for the Ink
which ran darker even than I
and which I could flood the world
with; for Temperance; for Faith

which lets me know what I must do,—
bend, bow my head and knee.
Be humble, so saieth Thee
and they, my family, who does not know
my *first* name. My quill feather flies

across the page. I wait.

AN HYMN TO THE MORNING

Faith for me is waking—
    a stitch in my neck
    or back,
But Awake—

Tho it is still dark.
    My job to walk
    through stark
Dawn and provide a Spark—

I feel like
    words not
    fully known yet,
Like *Electric*—

The lanterns begin—
    brighten—
    and it is mine,
This time before Time,

The oil lamps' companion.
    Of soot born,
    of burn,
Child of sand and sun,—

Here, in this wooden house
    I take the gift to us
    from Prometheus—
For which he was Punish-

Ed, and made
    a slave—
    starved and chained
Against the Rock face—

And the cold lamps I light.
　　The shadows hide
　　my silhouette,
The low fires

By which I write—
　　God
　　that my hand
Guides—

Hear my song!
　　Here it is morning.
　　Approaching,
Our Day shall not be long—

ON THE AFFRAY IN KING-STREET, ON THE EVENING OF THE 5TH OF MARCH, 1770

Why not run? Like young
Crispus Attucks unmoored
from Framingham
to become a dockhand

lugging tea and rum.
Like a mouth his master ran
an ad offering a reward
for his return. Instead,

Attucks, once you're dead,
we will hoist your name
like a flag. The mob
had its orders, attacked,

the king his stones.
The lobster-coats
surely saw you, stevedore,
swaying there, a head taller

than anyone—they'd sparred
with you & others
just days before.
Death no one spares.

I've never heard a black man
loved so, by God—
through the streets
where slaves are sold

your name now rings
out like the cold, or coal
whistling in the fire.
One musket ball sped

through your spare rib.
The other through
your true. What all
you left behind:—

this pewter teapot,
dry, battered, parched,
without one dark drop.
Adam of us all,

you are buried
on a hill
where the stones
grow slowly small.

AUTOPSY

I, *Benjamin Church, Jun.*, of lawful age, testify and say,
that being requested by Mr. Robert Pierpont, the Coroner,
to assist in examining the body of Crispus Attucks, who
was supposed to be murdered by the soldiers

on Monday evening *the 5ᵗʰ instant*, I found two wounds
in the region of the thorax, the one on the right side,
which entered through the second true rib
within an inch and a half of the sternum, dividing

the rib and separating the cartilaginous extremity from
    the sternum,—
the ball passed obliquely downward through the diaphragm
and entering through the large lobe of the liver and the gall-
    bladder,
still keeping its oblique direction, divided the aorta descendens

just above its division into the iliacs, from thence it made its exit
on the left side of the spine. This wound I apprehended
was the immediate cause of his death.
The other ball entered the *fourth* of the false ribs,

about five inches from the linea alba, and descending *obliquely*
passed through the second false rib, at the distance of about
eight inches from the linea alba; from the oblique direction
of the wounds, I apprehend the gun must have been discharged

from some *elevation,* and further the deponent saith not.

EXAMINATION

Misery is often the parent of the most affecting touches in poetry.
—Among the blacks is misery enough, God knows, but no poetry.
—THOMAS JEFFERSON
Notes on the State of Virginia

Taken apart, dissected, held
up to the oily light—
through your pages men look
and poke, as if to see something lying

in wait, deceit or disease.
Your best hope is hoax.
Who in the Colonies would believe
all this you say you wrote?

Mere Negress, a girl
forever,—it's true however
you were still
mostly a girl, nineteen by our

best judgement. And judge
we did:—asked you to speak
the Lord's Prayer, catechisms
we later made you write

down while we watched. Who
do your words
belong to? Without ours
yours are no one's—tho

perhaps belong to Messr. Wheatley
who still claims they
are your own. Even a parrot may
recite, but can a monkey write?

We have become convinced, by study
and questioning, to the best
of our ability,
of your words' origin—Wheatley,

he does not lie. I see no reason
why we the Committee should not
grant this book the right
to publication, not as fiction

but as exhortation, a Declaration
that God has blessed
this black with a mind. I do not
mind listing you

among the creatures of old wives
and myth. Like Tituba the witch
you have told what it is
you have seen, tho thankfully

no devils. Like Attucks you'll die
for wars we wage like sin
to secure our freedom. I cannot
find any evidence to dispute

this slave girl's authorship
and place here my imprint.

ON THE DEATH OF THE REV.
MR. GEORGE WHITEFIELD, 1770

An ELEGIAC POEM, On the DEATH
of that celebrated Divine,
and eminent Servant

of JESUS CHRIST, the late
Reverend, and pious George Whitefield,
Chaplain to the Right

Honourable the Countess
of Huntingdon, &c &c.
Who made his exit from this transitory

State, to dwell in the celestial
Realms of Bliss, on LORD's DAY,
30th of September, 1770, when he was seiz'd

with a Fit of the Asthma,
at NEWBURY-PORT,
near Boston, in New-England,

In which is a Condolatory
Address to His truly noble
Benefactress

the worthy and pious Lady
HUNTINGDON,—and the Orphan-Children
in GEORGIA; who, with many

Thousands, are left, by the Death
of this great man, to lament
the Loss of a Father, Friend,

and Benefactor,
By PHILLIS, a Servant
Girl of 17 Years of Age, belonging

to Mr. J. WHEATLEY, of Boston:—
And has been
but 9 Years from Africa

in this country.

TO MR. AND MRS. ————,
ON THE DEATH OF THEIR INFANT SON

Whatever the hour carried
On that brilliant grey day
When you married you made
The most of,—a quiet kiss, a cry.

No one threw rice. It was
All you could afford, the clothes
And the pastor secondhand—
Inherited like you had

Your freedom once the Mistress
(you wept) grew sick and passed.
Months later you lost your *first*:—

His small fluttering chest
Like a bird far fallen from the nest.
His shy head the size of your opening fist.

EMANCIPATION

Freedom for me means rising up
early, to sweep and clean the chamber
pots of strangers,—this house
boards many men who manage

never to see me:—I am no language
they know, or I let them think so.
It is worse if one has heard
of me somehow, if the papers run

my elegies, or print on this new nation
my praises. I sleep beneath the stair
dreaming the risers stars, run
lines thro my head like a poor

pastor, or understudy. I write
when time I can spare, wonder:—
Lord, why was I spared? Times
like this I miss my Mistress

who fed and taught me to read
God's word—now dead
(so set me free), she still speaks
often to me—discouraged

my marrying, her spirit still unwilling
tho I own my freedom. My body weak.
From Britain's bosom, lionized,
I returned just in time to hear

the first shots, for Revere to ride
through town and Crispus Attucks
to embrace the muskets.
That seems long ago indeed—

my mistress having called me
back home, to her, then the Lord
summoning her to Him.
Like prayer I cleaved to her side.

Whether martyr or maid
you die and join with God,
you hope—your name written
deep enough and dark

it will not be forgot.

ELEGY ON LEAVING ———

Presented with *Paradise*
Lost in London by the mayor
your first (and last)
triumphant trip there

you read Milton with care, knew
his Devil not as talk, or fast hands,
but silence:—your words that no longer
arrive, your husband in debtor's

prison to pay off first the house
on Queen Street (your envious
neighbors), then on Prince
where your third colic

breathing babe grew cold
and passed. (Where hours after
you met your Lord.)
Your beloved

copy (and you only 31 years old)
of *Paradise Lost*, to eat, long sold.

MASSACHUSETTS INDEPENDENT CHRONICLE AND UNIVERSAL ADVERTISER, 8 DECEMBER 1784

NOTICES:

The body of the young Lady, lost
in Capt. Copeland's sloop

on Cohasset rocks, as late-
ly mentioned in this paper,

has since been found, and
decently interred.

SHIPS ENTERED:

MARRIED, at her Father's Mansion,
in Duxbury, by the Reverend
Mr. Sanger, the amiable

Miss NABBY ALDEN, youngest Daughter
of Colonel Briggs Alden, of that Place,
to Mr. BEZA HAYWARD, of Bridgewater.

SHIPS CLEARED:

Last Lord's day died,
Mrs. PHILLIS
PETERS (formerly Phillis
Wheatly) aged 31, known

to the literary world
by her celebrated miscellaneous
Poems. Her funeral is
to be this afternoon, at 4 o'

clock, from the house lately improved
by Mr. Todd, nearly opposite
Dr. Bulfinch's, at West-
Boston, where her friends

and acquaintances are desired
to attend. *(No one did.)*

A FAREWEL TO AMERICA

On Her Maiden Voyage to England

There are days I can understand
why you would want to board
broad back of some ship
and sail: venture, not homeward
but toward Civilization's

Cold seat,—having from wild
been stolen, and sent into more wild
of Columbia, our exiles
and Christians clamoring upon
the cobblestones of Bostontown—

Sail cross an Atlantic (this time) mild,
the ship's polite and consumptive
passengers proud. Your sickness
quit soon as you disembarked in mist
of London—free, finally, of our Republic's

Rough clime, its late converts who thought
they would not die, or die simply
in struggle, martyr to some God,—
you know of gods there
are many, who is really only

One—and that sleep, restless fever
would take most you loved. Why
fate fight? Death, dark mistress,
would come a-heralding silent
the streets,—no door to her closed,

No stair (servant, or front) too steep.
Even Gen. Washington, whom you praise,
victorious, knows this—will even admit
you to his parlor. Who could resist a Negress
who can recite Latin and speak the Queen's?

Docked among the fog and slight sun
of London, you know who you are not
but that is little new. Native
of nowhere—you'll stay a spell, return,
write, grow still. I wake with you

In my mind, leaning, learning
to write—your slight profile
that long pull of lower lip, its pout
proving you rescued by
some sadness too large to name.

My Most Excellence, my quill
and ink lady, you scrawl such script
no translation it needs—
your need is what's missing, unwritten
wish to cross back but not back

Into that land (for you) of the dead—
you want to see from above
deck the sea, to pluck from wind
a sense no Land can
give: drifting, looking not

For Leviathan's breath, nor for waves
made of tea, nor for mermen half-
out of water (as you)—down
in the deep is not the narwhal enough real?
Beneath our wind-whipt banner you smile

At Sea which owns no country.

from

DEAR DARKNESS

POEMS

{ 2008 }

for my father
Paul E. Young
"BRUDDA"
1942–2004

and my grandmother
Joyce Pitre Young
"MUDDA"
1921–2004

NINETEEN SEVENTY-FIVE

Since there was no better color
or name, we called the dog
Blackie, insurance no one would forget
the obvious. One of the few dark ones
in the bunch, the only male,
he died twelve human years later
standing on a vet's table—
when the news came Mama
Annie, visiting, gathered us
in a circle of hands, called up
Jesus to the touch, to protect.

But that year when beautiful
still meant Black, when I carried
home my first dog full of whimpers
& sudden dukey, we warmed him
in our basement with a bottle disguised
as his mother, we let his hair grow long
around his feet, just as ours did

around ears, unbent necks. Back
in the day, my mother cut my afro
every few months, bathroom layered
with headlines proclaiming the world's end,
our revolution. I cannot recall
when I first stepped into the reclining
thrones of the barbershop
when I first demanded to go there alone,
motherless, past the spinning white
& red sign left over from days of giving
blood, to ask for my head turned
clean, shorn, for the cold to hold.

I only remember how back then the room
seemed to fill with darkness as she trimmed
my globe of hair, curls falling like an earth
I never thought would be anywhere
but at my feet, how the scissors twanged
by these ears like the raised voice
of a Southern gentleman the moment after
some beautiful boy segregates coffee, no cream,
black, onto his creased & bleached lap.

TUFF BUDDIES

for Robert Scott

No sign or behind warming
could keep us from careening
down hills or popping wheelies;
the blue brake on our Big
Wheels only helped us peel
out, skid. Robert & I were Tuff
Buddies, friends for life, two kids
thrown together like the sandbox
& swings our fathers put up
in the gap between buildings.
We dug & played but mostly
sailed down Buswell Street
on those glorified tricycles souped
up our own way, ripping off
hokey handle-ribbons that fanned
useless, bicentennial. We removed
the blue, low-backed safety
seat, then conveniently lost it—better
able to stand for jumps, dismounts,
we'd hit the raised ramp at hill's bottom
then leap & pray the same way Robert,
Superdog, & I once spilled out a red
wagon right before it swerved, then
plunged through the garage
of my new house. Beyond
that patched hole our hides paid for
my Big Wheel still rots. I wouldn't let
them sell it with the yard; I still love
the wheels' blue click, black scrape
of plastic tire on the walk. I guess
I'm still holding on some to days
like that, still counting ten

———————

like when D Doc would come over, greet
Robert & me with a handshake, counting
out loud, clenching our fingers to what
we thought death. Whoever lasted
got a half-dollar & we somehow always
made it, miraculous. What did I know
then of love but licorice & the slow
Sunday smell of the drugstore
Doc built up himself, his wife GiGi's
church-long hugs? It was years before
I heard his real name or learned
he wasn't kin, more till someone
mentioned West Indian. Always
the gentleman, one of the first I loved
to die, his lean voice confessed that spring
the chemo was over—*Don't know
son, this stuff, it's got me by the bones.*
Mostly, I remember his hands large
numbing mine, numbering, at the end
sounding almost surprised—*My,*
he'd say, *you're quite the grown
fellow*—then his letting go.

AUNTIES

There's a way a woman
         will not
relinquish

her pocketbook
         even pulled
onstage, or called up

to the pulpit—
         there's a way only
your Auntie can make it

taste right—
         rice & gravy
is a meal

if my late Great Aunt
         Toota makes it—
Aunts cook like

there's no tomorrow
         & they're right.
Too hot

is how my Aunt Tuddie
         peppers everything,
her name given

by my father, four, seeing
         her smiling in her crib.
There's a barrel

full of rainwater
         beside the house
that my infant father will fall

into, trying to see
         himself—the bottom—
& there's his sister

Margie yanking him out
         by his hair grown long
as superstition. Never mind

the flyswatter they chase you
         round the house
& into the yard with

ready to whup the daylights
         out of you—
that's only a threat—

Aunties will fix you
         potato salad
& save

you some. Godmothers,
         godsends,
Aunts smoke like

it's going out of style—
         & it is—
make even gold

teeth look right, shining,
         saying *I'll be
John,* with a sigh. Make way

out of no way—
         keep the key
to the scale that weighed

the cotton, the cane
    we raised more
than our share of—

If not them, then who
    will win heaven?
holding tight

to their pocketbooks
    at the pearly gates
just in case.

from **PALLBEARING**

PALLBEARING

In the end it all

comes to this—
wigs & rosaries
folks bent to knees

first time in years
God blond above
the casket

& no one singing
or saying a thing—
men holding

their hats, uncut hair
keeping porkpie shapes
some with smiles

& kisses for widows—
the clumsy crosses
hands old or amnesiac

make—folks laying
hands on the body
as if to heal—this

goodbye is gone
& we line up
to lift, a grand-

son's duty, bearing
the pall, like Paul
—my father's name

though few call him that—
following the hearse
lights low cross

water knee deep
in the road, a sea
no Moses can part—

rain no Noah's
seen for years—
I'm a get them niggahs

my Auntie says Da Da
dead, must have said,
making sure

there wouldn't be
too much drinking
& carrying on

over him. Da Da,
along the road
from the wake

to the grave, that black
dog could be you
sniffing at sugar cane

fallen from trucks—
a struck possum
on the shoulder—

At the burial site your weight
is mine—I toss white
gloves in the grave

before it's filled
& the saints go
marching past—

On the way back
to the house & the repast
& whatever else awaits

I still
bear you, lift you up
over fields, over cypress

& song The Kingpins
Baby
It'll Be Alright

from the radio
next to distant cousins
barbequeing for us

Brudda—my father—
sees the dark circling
looks up & says Never

seen this many
crows in all
my days—

VICTUALS

He is dead so we eat.
In his heaven he must be
hungry—so we fill
ourselves, stomachs,

for him—the red sauce
& the meat, acres
of pies Aunties have
blessed. In the yard kin-

folk I've never met
open the giant barrel grill
& smoke seeps out
the lid. He is dead. Bury

our faces in food
to forget, in vain, the rain
falling, fallen, water standing
like he never again.

EULOGY

All talk
is lucky. Just ask
my grandpere, growing
into earth, half-

French, all man-
drake screaming when pulled
from its roots. (You need
a dog to undo it properly, staying

just out of earshot.)
Below us he hears
as the dead must, the day
speaking to itself, muttering

as he did, going deaf—
from him sounds retreat
as if beneath great
water. The Gulf. The coin

on his tongue drug
him down. I do say—
I loved him. Lucky
to have told him. Our talk

black cats crossing
the path—rare
& dangerous. Don't give me
any lip. No jazz. Don't ask

me to say it any
better than this—our last
and only kiss, butterflies

fluttering shut like mouths
above him.

SEE THAT MY GRAVE
IS KEPT CLEAN

Lost in the heat
we search the colored section
of the town cemetery

for my great-
grandfather's grave—
find only crumbling names

that sound French
& familiar, none
his. Deep weeds. Jesus

a statue facing just
the white stones—
crucified high above,

his back to us.

INSURANCE

Dependable as death, the white man
knocked each month, called
Mudda by her first name

& collected the next installment
for her burial. She paid
for her death fifty

times over, not just
in money, but if
you were there you'd see

that while he called her
Joycie
& she hunted for the money

she didn't have, had somehow
set aside, my grandmother shot
him a look

that if you knew
her, & only if,
was the opposite

of affection—pity
perhaps, but more
like the disregard

the world had tried
tossing her way
& had failed. Even

his *Thanks kindly*
or *See you next month*
couldn't counter

her long stare after
he let the screen door
slam shut, rusty springs

tsk-tsking behind him.

CASTING

I learned to shoot
that summer in Maine
my father studying
medicine & teaching
me what he called
survival. I sent BB's
or stones from a sling
through beer cans as
aluminum as the canoe
I figured out how
to row, each hole
an aim, exclamation.

Mornings, before seminars
on blindness & open
hearts, my father
taught me targets
& fishing: his unshaking
surgeon hands would thread
a hook, worm it, then cast out
like a leper, the pole
his unsteady crutch.
Gnats circled like verbs.
Dad paced that rotting

dock, threatening to cast
me in the lake—that'd
show me to swim all
right, and how.
That night I dreamt
the rental house
into water, woke
to wade among lures
leaned dark against
door frames, reeling
among what deep
I couldn't breathe.

Next morning, the trout
I yanked from the grey-green
lake stared back like the lung
it didn't have, mouth
opening & closed
in prayer, a dank flag
lifted feet free
of water I feared,
that damp even
my dog dared enter.

In the picture I look
happy as a trigger
holding the prize rainbow
high: dog, Dad, & me
glittering big as the fish,
rod & line stitching
us together like
the birthmark a doctor
removed so young
now only my slight,
side scar remembers.

BLACK CAT BLUES

I showed up for jury duty—
turns out the one on trial was me.

Paid me for my time & still
I couldn't make bail.

Judge that showed up
was my ex-wife.

Now that was some
hard time.

She sentenced me
to remarry.

I chose firing squad instead.
Wouldn't you know it—

Plenty of volunteers
to take the first shot

But no one wanted to spring
for the bullets.

Governor commuted my term to life
in a cell more comfortable

Than this here skin
I been living in.

SOMETHING BORROWED BLUES

I finally found me
a nice girl

to marry—
I thought she'd been voted

Most Likely
& Pretty

turns out she
was voted Most Pity.

Went on down to the courthouse
& the test said

we were kin—
not blood

but same proof
of liquor stained our veins.

We eloped
anyway.

Her mama's name
was Backhand

& her daddy
called Jalopy—

they couldn't give her away.
She had her a voice

like an axe
& danced

like a pickup
wrecked beside the road.

We spent our honeymoon
at home

since hell was booked
till who knows.

FLASH FLOOD BLUES

I'm the African American
sheep of the family.

I got my master's
degree in slavery.

Immigrant
to the American dream,

Evacuee,
I seen the water

Ladder its way
above me. Swam

To the savings & loan—
no one home.

I've steered
Hardship so long—

Even my wages of sin
been garnished.

Wolf tickets
half off.

Collect call
& response.

Whenever we pass
on the street

Death pretends
not to know me

Though the grapevine say
he's my daddy.

LIME LIGHT BLUES

I have been known
   to wear white shoes
beyond Labor Day.
   I can see through
doors & walls
   made of glass.
I'm in an anger
   encouragement class.
When I walk
   over the water
of parking lots
   car doors lock—
When I wander
   or enter the elevator
women snap
   their pocketbooks
shut, clutch
   their handbags close.
Plainclothes
   cops follow me in stores
asking me to holler
   if I need any help.
I can get a rise—
   am able to cause
patrolmen to stop
   & second look—
Any drugs in the trunk?
   Civilian teens
beg me for green,
   where to score
around here.
   When I dance,
which is often,
   the moon above me
wheels its disco lights—

until there's a fight.
Crowds gather
    & wonder how
the spotlight sounds—
    like a body
being born, like the blare
    of car horns
as I cross
    the street unlooking,
slow. I know all
    a movie needs
is me
    shouting at the screen
from the balcony. From such
    heights I watch
the darkness gather.
    What pressure
my blood is under.

ODE TO THE MIDWEST

The country I come from
Is called the Midwest
—BOB DYLAN

I want to be doused
in cheese

& fried. I want
to wander

the aisles, my heart's
supermarket stocked high

as cholesterol. I want to die
wearing a sweatsuit—

I want to live
forever in a Christmas sweater,

a teddy bear nursing
off the front. I want to write

a check in the express lane.
I want to scrape

my driveway clean

myself, early, before
anyone's awake—

that'll put em to shame—
I want to see what the sun

sees before it tells
the snow to go. I want to be

the only black person I know.

I want to throw
out my back & not

complain about it.
I wanta drive

two blocks. Why walk—

I want love, n stuff—

I want to cut
my sutures myself.

I want to jog
down to the river

& make it my bed—

I want to walk
its muddy banks

& make me a withdrawal.

I tried jumping in,
found it frozen—

I'll go home, I guess,
to my rooms where the moon

changes & shines
like television.

ODE TO THE SOUTH

I want to be soused,
doused

in gasoline
& fried,

fired up like a grill—

Let's   get   fired   up
We   are   fired   up

—I want to squeal
like a pig

or its skin. Gridiron.
Pork rind.

I want to be black
on the weekend—

I want God to root
for the home team.

I want to flood
my greens in vinegar

please.
I want everyone

to be named *man*.
Yes ma'am.

I want my cake
& to barbeque, too.

Propane, diesel,
rocket fuel—

It's not the heat it's
the hospitality.

I want to pray
on game day.

I want to sweat

in the shower,
to *shoot*

when I could say
somethin worse

like Jesus. I want a grill
of gold

& a God that tells

the truth, who sleeps
late on Sunday

& lets church out early
so I can make

the buffet.
I want the preacher to go late.

I want to give God
a nickname.

UNCLES (BLOOD)

Talk turns
to who has the sugar
& how much water
you should drink a day,
to conspiracy theories—*cornbread
can kill you*—

Uncles give advice
not gifts. They forget
your birthday but recall
how short you once were
forever. In your mind
they always loom taller

even years after bumping you
the Bar-Kays from an 8-track—
all bass & bucket seats
in the souped-up black Camaro
parked in the yard
they mean to mow.

Uncles will build half
a house, the frame, the place
the plumbing will go, all
beam & bone,
& never finish the walls

till one day the rain will
rot it all.
Uncles got plans
& they're big.
Uncles underestimate

everything but food, buy
in bulk then watch it
go bad. Uncles heal
with a touch & can fry
turkeys whole. Uncles smoke
menthols & speak

prophecy. Will lift
you above their head,
bad backs & all—will jerry-rig
a motor to an old-fashioned
lawnmower to slay

the weeds. Will lie
down after, exhausted,
prone on Mama's couch,
refusing to see

no doctor—dragged in
lucky, Doc'll say, hours before
shrapnel from some unseen
mowed-over tin
was about to bore

into their huge hearts.
Uncles lie
beautifully. Years later
Uncles won't much remember—
instead show you their watch

that's stopped—*It's ghetto,*
they'll laugh, flashing teeth
more gold than their timepiece
that's a copy
of a copy of a copy—
the battery run down

but still worn, still shiny.

ODE TO PORK

I wouldn't be here
without you. Without you
I'd be umpteen
pounds lighter & a lot
less alive. You stuck
round my ribs even
when I treated you like a dog
dirty, I dare not eat.
I know you're the blues
because loving you
may kill me—but still you
rock me down slow
as hamhocks on the stove.
Anyway you come
fried, cued, burnt
to within one inch
of your life I love. Babe,
I revere your every
nickname—bacon, chitlin,
cracklin, sin.
Some call you murder,
shame's stepsister—
then dress you up
& declare you white
& healthy, but you always
come back, sauced, to me.
Adam himself gave up
a rib to see yours
piled pink beside him.
Your heaven is the only one
worth wanting—
you keep me all night
cursing your four-
letter name, the next
begging for you again.

ODE TO CHICKEN

You are everything
to me. Frog legs,
rattlesnake, almost any
thing I put my mouth to
reminds me of you.
Folks always try
getting you to act
like you someone else—
nuggets, or tenders, fingers
you don't have—but even
your unmanicured feet
taste sweet. Too loud
in the yard, segregated
dark & light, you are
like a day self-contained—
your sunset skin puckers
like a kiss. Let others
put on airs—pigs graduate
to pork, bread
become toast, even beef
was once just bull
before it got them degrees—
but, even dead,
you keep your name
& head. You can make
anything of yourself,
you know—but prefer
to wake me early
in the cold, fix me breakfast
& dinner too, leave me
to fly for you.

ODE TO WILD GAME

My daddy died loving
you, had since
he was eight. High school
sweetheart, long distance
romance, it's you he missed
most months
of the year, kept you near
like a picture, packed away
& pulled out when you weren't
around to remind him
he was alive. Out,
into the wild, the world,
is where you led. He died
hunting after you, you
are like pity—always
too much of you, or not near
enough. I miss
the way he held you
& like time would not waste you.
Elusive mistress
he'd later marry, you were
the midwife of his late happiness
& he was born at home
with no spoon in his mouth,
no hammer in his hand,
just his hard head
I inherited. At this hour
I bet you fear
you were better off
dead, you widow of the field,
you father gone too soon—
my grandmother of all mercy

who's outlived
her only, full-grown son
& never mentions the first
one who died
long ago young.

ODE TO HOMEMADE WINE

You are stronger
than you think. Quiet
cousin of mine, my uncle
made you & never knew
till years later
when you knocked at his door
& called him *father*.
Even his wife welcomes
you home. We all
seem loud with you around.
You fix the front porch
so it no longer leans—
take out the sting
the day my daddy's buried,
talking trash
& laughing. *You crazy*,
he would have said,
which where I come from
is a compliment. Mother
of moonshine, you swore
to get the jalopy in the lawn
running again, may get
around to it yet.
Though cloudy, you know
better than anyone
that death, while hell,
may make folks better—
you keep just
this side of rotten.
For you we've had to come up
with new names—
fermented, brewed,
settling in—but, lucky
for us, no funds.
Slow to anger, quick

to act, you are
the house my father
was born in, only last year
torn down to stop
from falling on this one—
the child's chair my grandfather
or his father made,
rocking, wood, painted
a green that won't
quit blooming
but must have seemed
to most folks only old, tossed
behind the house to rot
with the blackberries. Saved,
shipped, shaken
free of mites, that rocker
I found after my father's
funeral is like you—rickety
yet sturdy, you always
do the trick. You never
beg, nor borrow, save
all pain for tomorrow.

ODE TO GRITS

Like *y'all,* or sorrows,
or pigsfeet,
or God, your name
always holds multitudes—
is never just one—

unlike *moose* or *deer*
or death—which means both many
& alone. Little Lazarus,
you're the world before
the flood, & what's after,

are ash turning back
to a body. Done wrong,
you are the flavor
of a communion wafer.
Miss Hominy,

for years I misheard
your name as *Harmony*
& I was right. Kissing cousin
to Cream of Wheat, godmother
to oatmeal, no one

owns you, much less
no Quaker. Those mornings
over Strawberry Quik
when the kettle called
the Cream of Wheat cook

to meet me for breakfast,
you waited patiently to shine
the whites of your million eyes
on me. You must know
I love you by the way

I like you plain, maybe
buttered up a bit.
Salty, you keep me
on my toes, let me
believe, this once,

in purity—no cheese,
no grape jelly, no Missus
Butterworth's. Undoctored,
your cloudy stare
unlike my father's, his one

eye no bullet met
that, hours after he was shot
through the other,
I had to decide to give over
to someone still

alive, some girl or old
man whose vision—
even dead, ever
the healer—my father saved.
Resurrected like you

are daily. Welcome
stranger, pennywise
prophet, you are the wet nurse
of mercy, the rock
water makes speak.

ODE TO CHITLINS

i.m. Charlie Barfield
1950–2007

How do you like them wrankles?
asks my uncle, parish
constable, four
hundred pounds if he's
an ounce, & my best
answer may be: *A lot.*

Wrinkled wise man,
you are the kind of kin
I trust few hands
to help with—like his wife my Auntie
Faye's, whose name might
as well be Faith, for that's
what lets me let her

bring you to me
bleached, boiled, run
through the washing machine
till clean. Sweetbread's
sister, tripe's long
lost cousin, you're the uncle
I one day learnt

wasn't really—but I have grown
old enough, & young, to know blood
& family ain't always the same—
so you, I claim. You fed me
when I would have withered
without you, you weather me
like little else. I place

my hands upon you, old
family friend, & pray
you're well the way
my blood-uncle phoned
to pray with me after
my father died, when all
I wanted was his best

brisket, smoked slow.
Pork loin's poor brother,
you visit once a year, come
Christmas, if we're lucky—lately
even less. No use
waiting, or complaining—
your guts

are glory. Though your birth
certificate may read *Chitterlings,*
only Holy Ghosts' baptism record
gets your name right, like it did
my daddy's. Despite what
the newspapers say, your name
is not short

for anything, needs
no apostrophe. Those tight jeans
you wear, the ones with creases
ironed in—your linen
suit in winter—are out
of style & you don't care
who knows it. The road may seem long at first

you whisper, but see how brief
it's grown? The trail
may be full of shit
but you can make music
of even that. The last
place you'd look, you're hog
heaven—hard

to get to, much less
clean, you're where
we all end up. You are the finale
of most everything, grow
better with time
& Pace picante. Priest

of the pig, monk
of all meat, you warn me
with your vows
of poverty
that cleanliness is next
to impossible, that inside
anything can sing.

ODE TO GREENS

You are never what you seem.
Like barbeque, you tell me time
doesn't matter, that all
things wait. You take long
as it takes. Wife
to worry, you can sit
forever, stewing, grown
angrier by the hour.
Like ribs you are better
the day after, when all
is forgiven. Death's daughter,
you are often cross—bitter
as mustard, sweet
when collared—yet no one
can make you lose
all your cool, what strength
you started with. Mama's
boy, medicine woman,
you tell me things end
far from where
they begin, that forgiven
is not always forgotten.
One day the waters will part.
One day my heart will stop & still
you'll be here dark
green as heaven.

SUNDAY DRIVE

I been called by God
to testify
against him.

And the heart in its hole
knocks trying
to get out.

Pretty cage.

Sorrow the plate
scraped clean—
it's neither the food

eaten too fast
to enjoy, nor the empty
plate, but

the scraping.
What a song.

All night
long the silence
singing. The moles

making their way
beneath me while I sleep.

And Houdini, who could
escape anything, all
he wanted was to find

a way to speak
with his dead mother, so spent

most his life
proving séances false.

Now that's love.

He died
because he wasn't ready.

Me, I'm secondhand
like sections in the bookstore

I never noticed before—
Mysteries, or Used
Philosophy.

Downtown a hotel declares
Welcome
Great West Casualty.

Why not
decide the road along the rise
past the drive-in

showing nothing

& the church sign on the fritz
flashing like lightning.

SAY WHEN

Some days there is nothing
of the blues
             I can use
so I put down
my pen & walk instead

humming *Memories*
of You by Louie
Armstrong—
             it won't be long
before I have forgotten

the words, & soon
enough the words

will have gone
& forgotten me—

the silence we all meet.

I guess at God—

             the road twisting east
or south toward
the quarries,
             fading light.

My body rejecting
my own heart.

Trees touching
above the buildings.

I want to raise
my face
to the blackboard sky—

forgetting how hard
it is for me
not to believe—

& scrawl my name
on a slate

no hand can erase.

BOOK RATE

It's getting harder
to live without

faith, or you,
or whatever

we choose to call
what calls

to us in the quiet.

The cat that sleeps
on my mailbox, yawning.

The sky dark
at noon & soon

snow salting the ground.

Days almost zero.

What this world is
isn't enough

& that's enough—
or must be.

Steady flurries.

I want to enter the earth
face first.

Hurry—

NEW ENGLAND ODE

i.m. Richard Newman
d. 2003

Straight-backed pews
painted white
Compost, not trash
Boston marriage
Public school or Private
Paper, not plastic
Frappe, not milkshake
or malted
Rotary, not roundabout
Where do you summer?
Native, native, tourist
My loneliness
study group meets Thursdays
Shore, coast, overfished
Soda, not pop
Wetlands, not swamp
No Sunday Sales
Irish Twins
I'm a vegetarian
though I still love lamb
Pulpits high up
Spas, bubblers,
dry cleansers
Pineapple fences
Red tide
Sparkling or still
Woodchucks, not groundhogs
My dog & I
are both on a diet
Pay at the counter
Do you smell fire?
This is our year
All we need

is some good pitching
The Begonia Club
Volvo Volvo Volvo
Volvo Honda Volvo
The town my great-
grandfather founded
is just a tiny one
Fans, not a/c
Indian pudding
Patriot's Day, Bunker
Hill Day, Evacuation Day,
Lime Rickey
Curse, not pennant
Hiss, not boo
Pews you unlatch
to climb into, then lock
shut behind you

AMEN

Belief in God is proof
people exist.

ODE TO THE HOTEL
NEAR THE CHILDREN'S HOSPITAL

Praise the restless beds
Praise the beds that do not adjust
 that won't lift the head to feed
 or lower for shots
 or blood
 or raise to watch the tinny TV
Praise the hotel TV that won't quit
 its murmur & holler
Praise visiting hours
Praise the room service
 that doesn't exist
 just the slow delivery to the front desk
 of cooling pizzas
 & brown bags leaky
 greasy & clear
Praise the vending machines
Praise the change
Praise the hot water
& the heat
 or the loud cool
 that helps the helpless sleep.

Praise the front desk
 who knows to wake
 Rm 120 when the hospital rings
Praise the silent phone
Praise the dark drawn
 by thick daytime curtains
 after long nights of waiting,
 awake.

Praise the waiting & then praise the nothing
    that's better than bad news
Praise the wakeup call
    at 6am
Praise the sleeping in

Praise the card hung on the door
    like a whisper
    lips pressed silent
Praise the stranger's hands
    that change the sweat of sheets
Praise the checking out

Praise the going home
    to beds unmade
    for days
Beds that won't resurrect
    or rise
that lie there like a child should
      sleeping, tubeless

Praise this mess
    that can be left

FARM TEAM

I'm sick of this century
already.

My pleasant things all
ashes are.

No horizon—you can tell
the sky & ground

apart only
by guessing.

Rookie mistake.
Misery

is the only company
that would hire me

& I learnt yesterday
I'm getting laid off.

I wish wrong

& too often.
My pension

long gone, my job farmed
out to someone

better at failing—
I've been trained

in nothing.
I have taken myself

apart in the dark—
put back

together like a soldier
in the rain—one gear

always left over.

I SHALL BE RELEASED

What we love
   will leave us

or is it
   we leave

what we love,
   I forget—

Today, belly
   full enough

to walk the block
   after all week

too cold
   outside to smile—

I think of you, warm
   in your underground room

reading the book
   of bone. It's hard going—

your body a dead
   language—

I've begun
   to feel, if not

hope then what
   comes just after—

or before—
   Let's not call it

regret, but
    this weight,

or weightlessness,
    or just

plain waiting.
    The ice wanting

again water.
    The streams of two planes

a cross fading.

I was so busy
    telling you this I forgot

to mention the sky—
    how in the dusk

its steely edges
    have just begun to rust.

I WALK THE LINE

The bags beneath
my eyes are packed

but won't leave—
neither can I—

My plane hit
by lightning.

So I check back into Vegas
feeling like late Elvis—

not broke but broken.
Hard to know

when you're sick
of this place, or just sick—

There's always roulette.

I only bet black.

Soon my money
gone like Johnny

Cash who left us
after a dozen almosts—

spinning the rigged wheel
like a tune.

In May, June went—then July,
August, & now Johnny

who we'll rename autumn after.
Sadder than

a wedding dress
in a thrift store—

Salvation's an army
& Sun the record

I once found Cash's face on
warped but still good

for 5 bucks.
Death does

a brisk business.
Checking out,

the next morning I thought
I saw God

playing the cheap slots, praying
he'll win

before he loses.

I give the wheel one last spin
playing the age

I'll soon be
if I'm lucky—

the age Jesus was
when his Daddy did him in—

& hit—

Dealer stacks chips & asks
Want to keep going?

My plane waiting
to fly me home again

I think hard a moment,
tip big, cash

out & split.

I HOPE IT RAINS AT MY FUNERAL

And fire. And sleet.
And cloud covering

Over everything.
And the cold.

Too soon—

And bargains
with the Devil later

You don't regret.

And begging.
And belief.

Why now Lord.

And snow sealing
shut your eyes.

Enough.

And pleading
with Death to dawdle.

An hour.
A fortune.

No matter how much—

And tomorrow
still the sun

Who quits for no one.

EVERYBODY KNOWS THIS IS NOWHERE

I have driven for miles with bottles
left on my roof—

for miles folks pointing
out warnings

I thought welcomes.
I have waved back.

The sound
of broken glass

follows me around
like a stray.

Good boy.
Stay—

And the whales
washing themselves

ashore
nothing can save—

all day blankets wet
their skin like we're taught

to put fires out.

And the volunteers pushing them
back out at high tide

sleep well, exhausted, even
proud—before forty more,

the same, days later pilot
themselves ashore again,

blowholes opening
and closing like fists.

And the sound.

And the fires out west
started by someone

lighting love letters
she didn't want—

turns out to be a lie.

Blue blue windows
behind the stars.

And what if they had
been people instead

of whales, my mother wonders,
would that many

gather to save us?

Just enough
light to read.

ON BEING THE ONLY BLACK PERSON
AT THE JOHNNY PAYCHECK CONCERT

The man in the American flag
dress shirt wants to pick
a fight. He's been grabbing
women & high-

fiving his buddies all night.
We're here in Nashville
on our Meat Tour, getting the four
food groups in: chicken,

barbeque, cheeseburger, pork
chop sandwich still on the bone—
served with a pickle on a bun
and a half-full bottle of A.1.

The boot store also sells songs.
Johnny Cash's *Big River*
rolled out half-dozen times
along music row—requests

& tips—before we line up
like shots of Tennessee
sour-mash whisky
to see BR5-49, band named

for the telephone exchange
on the opening of *Hee Haw*.
Back when television
had no backup & you had to stand

to change channels, for an addict
kid like me Saturday-night TV
meant waiting out Lawrence Welk,
& then Buck Owens jumping out

of the corn, Minnie Pearl's hat
with the price tag still on it
dangling like a toe tag
on a dead man. The jokes

I never did get. Still the music told
what gingham would not—
heartbreak & history, voices
where accents are assets—

Close enough
for country music—
those twilight hours before *Love*
Boat became *Fantasy Island*

just as before the band who know
more Hank Williams than Hank
himself did, dead
in the back of his car

still headed toward a gig,
we must endure
coulda-beens like Johnny
Paycheck, who the poster

pictures young, handsome,
& pissed. His backup,
expanding-waist band
vamps till Johnny huffs,

washed up
neat & bearded, onstage,
the two steps to the risers
sending him out of breath.

Even jail, & years
of hard living,
don't deserve such
ashen fate. Paycheck

bounces along his set, enters
songs late & gets out
early, always ending with
Thank you all very much

no matter the thin applause.
Smoker's cough. Everyone
restless to hear his #1 pop
& country hit—*Take This Job*

and Shove It—
& while I hit the head

more out of boredom
than need, Paycheck obliges,
grudging into it, tonight less
an anthem against the Man

than a ditty disappointed
in itself—behind him the band
noodles solos while Paycheck,
spent, graduate

of anger management,
phones in
his resignation. Almost
an afterthought—

no encore—whoops
from the American flag
now too drunk to stand
or dance, in a town

that tonight, to Johnny, soon
dead, must seem
Cash Only—for now
Paycheck simply

smiles *Goodnight*—
wheezes—*You're too kind.*

LAST DITCH BLUES

Even Death
don't want me.

Spiders in my shoes.

Even God.

I tried
drinking strychnine

Or going to sleep
neath the railroad ties—

Always the light
found me first.

The Law.

Put me under arrest
for assaulting a freight—

Disturbing what peace.

(Turns out it
was only strych-eight.)

Tired of digging
my own grave.

Tired.

Spiders in my shoes.

The paperboy only
sold me bad news.

And wet at that.

The obit page said:
Not Today.

The weather blue too.

Stones all in my shoes.

SERENADE

I wake to the cracked plate
of moon being thrown

across the room—
that'll fix me

for trying sleep.
Lately even night

has left me—
now even the machine

that makes the rain
has stopped sending

the sun away.
It is late,

or early, depending—

who's to say.
Who's to name

these ragged stars, this
light that waters

down the milky dark
before I down

it myself.
Sleep, I swear

there's no one else—
raise me up

in the near-night
& set me like

a tin toy to work,
clanking in the bare

broken bright.

ODE TO CATFISH

Old man,
despite your beard
& bald head
you still ain't old
enough to be dead—
you swim back
slipping through my hands
into the dark & I wake.
Even in dreams you are dead.
Your fresh, certain smell—
cornbread batter frying
in the pan—mornings still
fills my face
& I am glad. No matter
the pain it takes
to hold you, your barbs
& beard, you sustain me
& I wander
humming your hundred names—
brother, bullhead, paperskin, slick.
Remember the day, po boy,
you fried up catfish
with grits for breakfast, your mother
& sisters surrounding us
& you declared it
perfect? Sweet Jesus
you were right.
Fish hooks in my heart.
My plate full of bones
I'm scared to swallow.

PRAYER FOR BLACK-EYED PEAS

Humbly, I come to you now
O bruised lord, beautiful
wounded legume,
in this time of plague, in my
very need. Ugly angel,
for years I have forsaken
you come New Year's Day,
have meant to meet you
where you live & not
managed to. I gave you up
like an unfaithful lover, but still
you nag me like a mother.
Like the brother I don't have
I need you now to confide in,
my eyes & yours darkened
by worry, my baby
shoes bronzed & lost.
Awkward antidote,
bring me luck & whatever
else you choose & I'll bend low
to shore you up. Part
of me misses you, part knows
you'll never leave, the rest
wants you to hear my every
unproud prayer. Wounded
God of the Ground, Our Lady
of Perpetual Toil & Dark Luck,
harbor me & I pledge each
inch of my waist not to waste
you, to clean my plate
each January & like you
not look back. You are
like the rice & gravy my Great
Aunt Toota cooked—you need,
& I with you, nothing else.

Holy sister, you are my father
planted along the road
one mile from where he
was born, brought full
circle, almost. You, the visitation
I pray for & what vision
I got—not quite
my father's second sight.
My grandmother saying
she dreams of me
& he every night. *Every*
night. Every night.
Small book of hours, quiet
captain, you are our future
born blind, eyes swole shut,
or sewn.

ODE TO GUMBO

For weeks I have waited
for a day without death
or doubt. Instead
the sky set afire

or the flood
filling my face.
A stubborn drain
nothing can fix.

Every day death.
Every morning death
& every night
& evening

And each hour
a kind of winter—
all weather
is unkind. Too

hot, or cold
that creeps the bones.
Father, your face
a faith

I can no longer see.
Across the street
a dying, yet
still-standing tree.

✳

So why not
make a soup
of what's left? Why
not boil & chop

something outside
the mind—let us
welcome winter
for a few hours, even

in summer. Some
say Gumbo
starts with *filé*
or with *roux,* begins

with flour & water
making sure
not to burn. I know Gumbo
starts with sorrow—

with hands that cannot wait
but must—with okra
& a slow boil
& things that cannot

be taught, like grace.
Done right,
Gumbo lasts for days.
Done right, it will feed

you & not let go.
Like grief
you can eat & eat
& still plenty

left. Food
of the saints,
Gumbo will outlast
even us—like pity,

you will curse it
& still hope
for the wing
of chicken bobbed

up from below.
Like God
Gumbo is hard
to get right

& I don't bother
asking for it outside
my mother's house.
Like life, there's no one

way to do it,
& a hundred ways,
from here to Sunday,
to get it dead wrong.

*

Save all the songs.
I know none,
even this, that will
bring a father

back to his son.
Blood is thicker
than water under
any bridge

& Gumbo thicker
than that. It was
my father's mother
who taught mine how

to stir its dark mirror—
now it is me
who wishes to plumb
its secret

depths. Black
Angel, Madonna
of the Shadows,
Hail Mary strong

& dark as dirt,
Gumbo's scent fills
this house like silence
& tells me everything

has an afterlife, given
enough time & the right
touch. You need
okra, sausage, bones

of a bird, an entire
onion cut open
& wept over, stirring
cayenne in, till the end

burns the throat—
till we can amen
& pretend
such fiery

mercy is all we know.

ODE TO SWEET POTATO PIE

Caramel. Coffee cake.
Chocolate I don't much love
anyway. Tough taffy.

Anything with nuts.
Or raisins. Goobers.
Even my Aunt Dixie's

apple pie recipe
or the sweet potato pie
my mother makes sing.

Even heaven. Even Boston
cream pie, Key Lime,
Baked Alaska, dense

flourless torte covered in raspberries
like a Bronx cheer.
Sherbet, spelt right,

and sandwiches
made of ice cream, even mint
or coffee I never drink,

even sherry, and smooth port
pulled up from shipwrecks
preserved on the bottom of the sea—

all this, & more, I would give up
to have you here, pumpkin-
colored father, cooking

for me—your hungry oven
humming—just one
more minute

ODE TO HOT SAUCE

Your leaving tastes
of nothing. Numb,

I reach for you
to cover my tongue

like the burnt word
of God—surrender

all to you, my fiery
sacrifice. My father

never admitted anything
was too hot

for him, even as the sweat
drained down his forehead,

found his worn collar
& eyes. You make mine

water & even water
won't quench you.

Only bread bests you.
Only the earth cools

& quiets this leftover
life, lights

my open mouth.
These days I taste

only its roof—
my house

on fire, all the doors
locked, windows latched

like my heart. My heart.
Carve it out

& on the pyre—
after the witch hunt

& the devil's
trial, after repentance

& the bright
blaze of belief—

it will outlive even
the final flame.

This is why I take
your sweet sting

into my eyes
& mouth like turpentine, rise

& try to face
the furnace of the day.

ODE TO PEPPER VINEGAR

You sat in the tomb

of our family fridge
for years, without

fail. You were all

I wanted covering
my greens, satisfaction

I've since sought

for years in restaurants
which claimed soul, but neither

knew you nor

your vinegar prayer.
Baby brother

of bitterness, soothsayer,

you taught
me the difference between loss

& holding on. Next to the neon

of the maraschino cherries,
you floated & stayed

constant as a flame

on an unknown soldier's grave—
I never did know

how you got here

you just were. Adrift
in your mason jar

you were a briny bit of where

we came from, rusty lid
awaiting our touch

& tongue—you were faith

in the everyday, not rare
as the sugarcane

my grandparents sent north

come Christmas, drained
sweet & dry, delicious, gone

by New Year's—

no, you were nearer,
familiar, the thump

thump of an upright bass

or the brass
of a funeral band

bringing us home.

ODE TO BOUDIN

You are the chewing gum
of God. You are the reason
I know that skin
is only that, holds
more than it meets.
The heart of you is something
I don't quite get
but don't want to. Even
a fool like me can see
your broken
beauty, the way
out in this world where most
things disappear, driven
into ground, you are ground
already, & like rice
you rise. Drunken deacon,
sausage's half-brother,
jambalaya's baby mama,
you bring me back
to the beginning, to where things live
again. Homemade saviour,
you fed me the day
my father sat under flowers
white as the gloves of pallbearers
tossed on his bier.
Soon, hands will lower him
into ground richer
than even you.
For now, root of all
remembrance, your thick chain
sets me spinning, thinking
of how, like the small,
perfect, possible, silent soul
you spill out
like music, my daddy

dead, or grief,
or both—afterward his sisters
my aunts dancing
in the yard to a car radio
tuned to zydeco
beneath the pecan trees.

BLUE LAWS

DEAR DARKNESS OUTTAKES

{ 2007–2009 }

WHITE WAY BLUES

From home I ran away
& joined Broadway—

my job was to play
the dark each Monday. Nobody

noticed my backdoor entrance
before each performance.

When I smile
it means Ladies

& Gents, two minutes
to curtain. My mama

came to see me closing
& opening night, which sure

enough, were one
& the same. I always

wanted to see my name
in lights, not in the mouth

of the magistrate.
My debut was made

at Outlandish Baptist
starring as the frankincense

in the Christmas pageant.
Exit, stage fright.

Now nightly I'm paid
in tomatoes, tossed,

I pretend are applause, save
past their expiration date

& carve lanterns out of.

BODY BAG BLUES

The guitar
     has no God
that is why

    I picked it

or it me—
     throat
I can throttle—

    a broken bottle
held against the neck
     till it whines—

a belly
     to strum
thunder from—

    a murmur
or holler
     no church knows—

or is this a choir
     beneath my fingers
& blisters—

    welcome,
there is none
     —the guitar

even makes
     goodbyes good

& the dead moan.

DEAD DADDY BLUES

The weather says
Listen
My mother says Pray
I walk around looking
for the light all day

God says nothing
The river Why
don't you stay
I wait around, wait
for the start of the rain

My feet say Forget you
My hands say Never
We look for him
by firefly light
like the supposed summer

Old grief can't protect you
New sorrow
sails your way
Lately it stays evening
almost all day

YELLOW DOG BLUES

Your gravestone still
on back order.

The post office usually
sends me so happy—

not today, lined up
on the eve

of New Year's to pay
the last

of your debs I owe.

Even your yellowing obit
ain't paid for yet.

Beside me my fellow
American clutch bills

in a weary bouquet, to buy
money orders for rent.

Only the Tide
I buy is improved.

Walking home, a long dog
sniffs from stoop

to stoop, his face almost
human, beseeching—

his neck
jangling his number

& family name

like your dog tags
I found buried

in a drawer days after
we'd buried you, father—

a surprise to see you
listed *Catholic*

in a raised metal
I want even now

to rub raw
as a rosary.

That old yellow dog
raises its head

like a nosy neighbor or
a new year, nods

& is gone.

2007

from

ARDENCY

★

A CHRONICLE
OF THE Amistad REBELS

☞

BEING AN EPIC ACCOUNT OF
THE CAPTURE
OF THE SPANISH SCHOONER

AMISTAD,

BY THE AFRICANS ON BOARD;
THEIR VOYAGE AND CAPTURE
NEAR LONG ISLAND, NEW YORK; WITH
PHRENOLOGICAL STUDIES
OF SEVERAL OF THE SURVIVING AFRICANS

★

COMPILED FROM AUTHENTIC SOURCES BY

Kevin Lowell Young

{ 2011 }

for Mama Annie

Painter, paint me a crazy jail, mad water-color cells.
Poet, how old is suffering? Write it in a yellow lead.

{ BOB KAUFMAN }
Jail Poems

PREFACE.

In the summer of 1839, fifty-three Africans illegally sold in Havana mutinied on the schooner *Amistad* while being taken to Puerto Principe. The rebels, mostly men from the Mendi people of Sierra Leone, killed the captain and the cook but spared their masters to help steer toward the rising sun and Africa. For nearly two months, the would-be slaveowners rerouted by night until a navy brig captured the ship off the coast of Long Island. Authorities quickly threw the Africans in Connecticut jails while deciding either to return the men to their Spanish masters or award them as "salvage" to the U.S. sailors.

White abolitionists took up the case, converting the Mendi to Christianity and teaching them English in preparation for the trial. The book's first section, *Buzzard,* is in the voice of James Covey, twenty-year-old African interpreter for the imprisoned Mendi; *Correspondance* consists of the Mendi's letters and speeches from jail (and subsequent freedom); the third section, *Witness,* is a libretto spoken/sung by Cinque, leader of the rebellion.

James Covey.

JAMES COVEY, the interpreter for the Africans, is apparently about 20 years of age; was born at Benderi, in the Mendi country. His father was of Kon-no descent, and his mother Gissi. Covey was taken by three men, in the evening, from his parents' house, at Go-la-hung, whither they had removed when he was quite young. He was carried to the Bullom country, and sold as a slave to Ba-yi-mi, the king of the Bul-loms, who resided at Mani. He lived there for three years, and was employed to plant rice for the wife of Ba-yi-mi, who treated him with great kindness. He was sold to a Portuguese, living near Mani, who carried him, with 200 or 300 others to Lomboko, for the purpose of being transported to America. After staying in this place about one month, Covey was put on board a Portuguese slave-ship, which, after being out about four days from Lomboko, was captured by a British armed vessel, and carried into Sierra Leone. Covey thus obtained his freedom, and remained in this place five or six years, and was taught to read and write the English language, in the schools of the Church Missionary Society. Covey's original name was *Kaw-we-li*, which signifies, in Mendi, *war road*, i. e., a road dangerous to pass, for fear of being taken captive. His Christian name, James, was given him by Rev. J. W. Weeks, a Church Missionary, at Sierra Leone. In Nov., 1838, he enlisted as a sailor on board the British brig of war Buzzard, commanded by Captain Fitzgerald. It was on board this vessel, when at New York, in Oct., 1839, that James was found, amid some twenty native Africans, and by the kindness of captain Fitzgerald, his services as an interpreter were procured.

from **BUZZARD**

*And it came to pass at the end of forty days, that Noah opened
the window of the ark which he had made:*

*And he sent forth a raven, which went forth to and fro, until
the waters were dried up from the earth.*

{ GENESIS 8:6−7 }

EXODUS

Gabriel, Escalastio, Desiderio,—in the seas beneath
the States, names new & Christian fell around you
like the lash. Before slavery, ten suns from water open
as a wound, you say you belonged to nothing
but home. Your back bore only spirit's teeth, scars
that meant manhood. Such rites of passage
protected little:—with in one moon you fared

no better than a slaver's shifting cargo of looking
glasses, olives. Out of boredom or freedom
of movement, the crew took a poker from under bitter
plaintains,—carved Captain's F into Cabin Boy's shoulder.
Parched as you were, would you have sipped the rum
& gunpowder smeared in that wound to make sure
it would brand? A few mad, swollen tongues caught

the saltwater Cabin Boy's good arm tossed. Was it
sanity drove cousin Fu-li to edge over the casket
of fresh water, lend it his own throat? Catching
him wet-lipped, Captain's men fed home
the whip:—even now you can hear his skin part,
can tell how much his body was water, how much
spine was book, just asking to be opened, read.

ADVENT

You tell me you never answer to lion
or boy, tho the papers have called
you Jinqua, Singbe, Cinquez,
Sinner. You stay cold as ever
in your naked cell, refusing the grey
robes this Union wished you in.
I have seen enough heads read lately

to know yours will make even fools
famous, hands translating your body
in lectures, from podiums, where *such
an African skull, well-formed, is seldom
to be seen—doubtless in other circumstances
an honor to his race.* At sea, your masters
must have dreamt that crown would buy

them islands. They named you Joseph, step-
father to the Lord, slept & saw you bring Mary,
laboring, on a mule. How could they have known
your son across the sea whose name you confide
means God? They woke to the sounds of Xmas,
your cane knife opening the heads of lords
& mulattoes, like wisdom, molasses beneath stars.

QUESTIONING

Who among you knew the Crew
split after seeing Captain's head
spill open? Who heard the lashings
come undone, or saw the gripe
unhooked, the lifeboat slip silent
over the side? While you knived
who saw the scar their cutter

made in water, slashing a wake
toward horizon, unseeable
shore? Who beheld the *Christ*
in your master's mouths as they watched
the night grow arms & strike? Did you
swab the sticky deck? Count casualties
like the black stars drown in?

Did you expect to meet ardency,
that wanting of wind? Who supposed
the stern would slow, your seizing
break, or guessed your masters,
while you slept, sailed for Providence?
And who let your dead launch
overboard, thrown like a voice?

FRIENDSHIP

During the mutiny your Masters must have heard
Captain & his mulatto Messboy go down the way
such family should, fighting, each splash the black wax
sealing an envelope. *If it may please the court:*—tho hidden
behind hungry barrels, the traders still ordered that boy,
Antonio, to toss you bread & allegiance. You found
your owners scared as stowaways on that boat baptized

Friendship,—bound them in chains to give a taste
of a slave's thirst. For days the fools refused to believe
property could be so bold. It was as if the beds they'd made
love to, their favorite muskets, grew blue with waiting
& woke. Unvexed, they wrote strange script to hand
any ships chanced upon; you sunk such letters
of death, unswayed. You say you sent anchors over

the same way, hoping to cease your drift, then turn round
toward family. When your sunburnt enemy called the sea
too deep to stop, you dove down far as lungs & doubt allowed,
emerged only with handfuls of blind, angelic fish. Little choice
but spare the cretins to navigate by scorpion, twin:—let them
steer your fellowship of thieves, give them all the water
they please, free them from irons, only thing ever they shared.

WASHINGTON

You harbored the ship like a criminal, stole
ashore hungry. Even eastward of Providence
reports had drifted of the strange spook
ship:—most thot you pirates, skin
the flag you never flew,—black covering skulls
& bones, crossed. When you signed for food,
dogs, folks drew water polite as blinds, then

called the pigs. Only Green, freelance captain,
would trade you goods. Wanted to turn you in
to gold,—stopped since you promised more
on board. While he haggled, the *Washington* found
your ship flagless, drunk with sea moss,—
covered in rent bags & one recent corpse.
Lieutenant added it up:—slaves & a fortune

in salvage. He sent you to the 3-ft. hold where Cinque
filled his belt with gold, leapt over the side. Sank. Swam out
of reach, an hour, while the brig searched. Drowning
the necklaces, surrendered himself. Reeled in, manacled,
Cinque pictures the necktie party the G-men got planned:—
I shall be hanged, I think, every day,—tongue flapping
a weather-beaten banner, pants full of freedom, soilt.

EASTER

Father:—I regret not having
sent word sooner. Here the Mendi
have begun to crack my knuckles
in greeting, to trust my words
like birds settling back on the branch
of my tongue,—forked, divining.
They write & learn things

quick as death. This makes me good,
reminds me how you adopted
& raised me like the dead, learning me
to say *pardon* to every passing
soul. Still, my interpretations loom less
necessary daily. Every letter they send
a sail, drawing home near.

I fear most the waking, watching them
leave to discover their own sun
& country. My sir, must we stand
to bring up what deserts us? Too soon,
it seems, I must close. May my words
reach you in manners I never can, crossing
boundless blue between. Yours, I remain,—

MAROON

How I hated you, dear Antonio, when you sang
of good treatment by the same masters
who'd branded you. When before God & every
one you swore the Mendi craved white men's
brains. I think we all shook our skulls
as the court swallowed that shuffle & jive:—
here comes the judge, here go the usual

suspects. Called to the stand, I felt so African
& pure, knowing something of a homeland,
some former name. All you had, Cabin Boy,
was your broken Spanglish. I know now
you were leaving, had planned
escape for days. How I picture you today,—
the laughing buffalo boy, trading tricks & skins

with the Indians. Brer Antonio with the rabbit
smile, not one rebel or pale prosecutor
saw you disappear among hounded hills. No body
watched you unhook yourself, sail quietly off. How
I envy the manner you turned up missing, a tooth
darkening, then fallen away. How our tongues
change, exposed, explore that space you've made.

BROADWAY

At Broadway Tabernacle the abolitionists charge
half-dollar a head to view your Mendi zoo.
After the slideshow of Sierra Leone, they hold
spelling bees to show how far you've come.
I wish for a word I could become. If just one letter
would shift, *worship* turning *warship* . . . But little
Kale spells it right:—*Bless-ed are the pure at heart.*

Freed, you've grown used to belting hymns
at the drop of a hat, then passing the plate
about. Tonight will rake in enough
to buy your craft & ship your selves home.
I want to join your crew
like a church, catch the red-eye to Africa,—
or at least Death's ferry, stowing away

to heaven. Let out the pews you Mendi jig,—
a crowd gathers, gives—& the men stoop
for change to buy some thing beside soft
shoes. The high-collar Committee has you return
the cash, prefers sideshows only under steeples,
pomp under certain circumstance. No one asks
after me,—still I dance, secret, with in my skin.

SOUNDINGS

We set course as if a meal, aim
like prayer home. Our ship
a barque name of *Gentleman,*—
what we's become—booked
& bobbing the harbor. I board
unbelieving,—fearing Customs
will hone in & call us bucaniers,

book us for stealing ourselves.
Instead, the men sing God
by the monkey gaff. No flags fly. Christ,
our new Pilot, provides. Sent to set
the mission up, Steele hits his Good
Book with a thump. Says we
been saved. The boat rocks.

The men shed clothes & English
soon as we set foot on solid ground.
See shore. See Mendi run. Our skin
again ours, blackens, a taut drum.
Either loud or without
a sound, each passenger like a pigeon
takes wing,—hunted, homing.

REVELATIONS

Mother:—time you get this I shall have flown
these States all together. The Committee raised
money like Jesus or bread,—I convinced myself
& the anti-slavers I had nothing left here
but second-hand words. Mother, some days
I wonder about the one who isn't you,
the one who birthed me & calls me dead

or stolen. I hope tonight to smuggle myself
home the same way. Mother, in all my nightly
horses my feet finally touch ground
then my lips,—looking up, the men scatter,
leaving shadows where bodies stood
one breath before. Home for them is whatever
they become, tho my arms fail wings.

Mother, when this letter arrives I hope
to have it told you already, your face & the trees
reminding us that wind drags words
far behind bodies. My words the barnacles
clutching ship's wood, helpless, helping
themselves. Wait & they will spring
geese from my mouth. In Christ & haste,—

3 feet 3 in. high

[The above engraving shows the position as described by Cingue and his compan-
ions, in which they were confined on board the slaver, during their passage from Af-
rica. The space between the decks represented in the engraving is three feet three
inches, being an actual measurement from a slave vessel. The space in the vessel
that brought the Amistad captives to Havana was, according to their statement,
somewhat larger, being about four feet between the decks.]

from **CORRESPONDANCE**

Canst thou draw out leviathan with an hook?
or his tongue with a cord *which* thou lettest down?

Canst thou put an hook into his nose? or bore his
jaw through with a thorn?

Will he make many supplications unto thee? will he
speak soft *words* unto thee?

Will he make a covenant with thee? wilt thou take
him for a servant for ever?

Wilt thou play with him as *with* a bird? or wilt thou
bind him for thy maidens?

Shall the companions make a banquet of him? shall
they part him among the merchants?

Canst thou fill his skin with barbed irons? Or his
head with fish spears?

Lay thine hand upon him, remember the battle,
do no more.

{ JOB 41:1–8 }

WESTVILLE

October 30, 1840

dear Sir   Mr tappan

   I want tell you Some thing   I going to write you a letter   I will write you
a few lines my friend   I am began to write you a letter   I bless you because
I love you   I want pray for you every night and every morning and evening
and I want love you too much   I will write letter for you from that time
Jesus began to preach and say repent   for the kingdom of heaven is at
hand   My Dear friend I thanks you a plenty because you Send me letter
and I thank you for it and I want pray for you every evening and every
night and every morning by day and by night and his always

   Mr Tappin   Love us   pray our father who art in heaven hallowed be
I want to tell you Some thing   I have no hat   Dear Sir I write you
if you please and so kind I please you   that I please you Let me have A hat to
cover my head   that I please you dear friend I tell you Some thing   I please
you that you let me have A bible   my friend I want you give me A hat
and I thank you a plenty   and I have no bible and hat both

   my friend I give you good loves   I believe you are my friend   my Sir I
want you tell your friends my good loves   I want love all teachers who
teach me and all my people good things about Jesus Christ God and heaven
and every things   I bless them that teach me good   I pray for them I want
write some   your name   thy kingdom come thy will be done in earth as it is
in heaven give us this day our daily bread and forgive us our debts as we
forgive forgive our debtors for thine is the kingdom and the power
and the glory for ever Amen   O Lord   my friend I write this paper to you
because I love you too much   my Sir   I want to tell you Some thing

   When we in havana vessel we have no water to drink   when we eat rice
white man no give us to drink   when Sun Set white men give us little water
when we in havana vessel white men give rice to all who no eat   fast he
take whip you   a plenty of them died and havana men take them put in
water   I try to write letter of paper for Mr you   and Jesus said unto him No

man having put his hand to the plough and looking back is fit for
the kingdom of God   my friend I am Stop writing your letter   Gone To you
a letter   my name Kale   I am your friend   I give you this letter

SPEECH

having English now
I hope to tell you what
it meant to hear your
words it was a river
slowly icing over it was
rain falling into water
was the night following
rain into water a father
crocodile waking early
to eat his children it
became the memory

of a gourd at my lips
the salt surrounding
the ship so white
& useless it was a thirst
a message thrown over
board a bottle a sudden
ash upon our skin our
tongues grown dark
& unavoidable as bay
leaves I thank you gentle
men for lending us yours

January 4, 1841

Dear Friend Mr. Adams,

I want to write a letter to you because you love Mendi
people and you talk to the grand court. We want to tell you
one thing; stranger say we born in Havana, he tell lie. We stay
in Havana 10 days and 10 nights, we stay no more. We all
born in Mendi. Mendi people been in Merica 17 moons. We
write every day; we write plenty letters; we read most all
ways; we read Matthew, and Mark, and Luke, and John,
and plenty of little books. We love books very much.

We want you to ask the court what we have done wrong. What
for Mericans keep us in prison? Some men say Mendi people
very happy because they laugh and have plenty to eat. No body
give Mendi people any these things. Mr. Judge come with bars
and sentences and Mendi people all look sorry. O we can't tell
how sorry. Some people say Mendi people no got souls, white
men afraid of Mendi people. Then we laugh. Why we feel bad
we got no souls?

Dear friend Mr. Quincy, you have children, you have
friends, you love them, you feel very sorry if Mendi people come
and carry them all to Africa. When Mr. Jailer came hear with
chains he put on some hands and he whip them to hard, he no feel
a shame. We afraid for Merica people because Merica people say
we make you free. If Merica people give us free we glad, if they no
give us free we sorry; sorry for Mendi people little; sorry for Merica
people great deal because God punish liars.

We want you to tell the court that Mendi people no want to go back
to New Havana, we no want to be killed. Dear friend you tell our Judges
let us free. Dear friend we want to know how we feel. Mendi people
think, think, think. No body know what we think. We think we know

God punish us if we have lie. We never tell lie; we fill truth. What for
Mendi people afraid? Because they got souls.

Cook says he kill, he eat Mendi people;
we afraid; we kill cook. Then captain kill one man with knife, and lick
Mendi people plenty. We never kill captain, he kill us. If court ask who
brought Mendi people to Merica? We bring ourselves. We hold
the rudder. All we want is make us free.

This from my hand,
Kin-na

TESTIMONY

You call us rebels   we were spoons
in that ship for so long   the wood
dark, drowned as the men who
made it from song   sold on land
like ships   like us   christened
out of water   You call us rebels
we were thrown with schools of fish
in the stomach of that ship   we slept
with the dead   which is not at all
You call us rebels   one day we took
the wheel from men with eyes of
water   we turned the ship towards
the rising sun   let the wind grace
our backs   that night we slept like
anchors   that night the sailors
turned us towards a Newborn
England   in dawn we saw blesséd
land   then felt the sun's heat
betraying our backs   too late
we saw the sunless men   their navy
racing   to rescue us into chains
now we know the edge of setting
sun   where only the dead are free
to come and go as you please

April 1, 1841

Dear Friend
Mr. L. Tappan

 I embrace this opportunity of writing a few
lines to you to inform you that I am well & when
this come to your hand & I hope that it may find you
in good health & yesterday our Judge set little
girls free & we are thankful & girls have free
now & I hope great God will bless you & keep
those who want hurt you

 & Tuesday night I wish & thank you very much
because you make us free & Mr Adams he made us
free & Menda people thank you very much I pray for you
& I am sorry to hear your Children have sick I hope God
to make them get well & I hope great God will bless you
& be my dear benefactory

 & I will pray for you when I go to bed and when
you rise in the morning & when you go to bed & what
we want you to do will you do it & I call you Dear Father
because you so kind to poor Menda & I wish pray to great
God to send us to our home he sent his Son to the world
to save us from going down to held

 all men have some work to do & suppose you must
let us go home & tell them about you jesus said unto him
foxes have holes & birds of the air have nests but the son
of man hath not where to lay his head My friend I want
you to carry us into Sierra Leone

 & this from your friend
Banna

CON.

President Tyler:

You have done a great deal
for us. Now we want to go home, very
much, very soon. When we get to Sierra
Leone, we get home, we find a good
place for our teachers, then tell enemies
and friends come see them. We want
plenty of calicoes, not cut, for men's coats,
pantaloons. For we think we wear Merica
dress as long as we live. We want plenty
to give our friends and have them give
us elephant teeth, camwood, palm
oil, and other things to send you
to Merica. We will take good care
of our teachers. We will not
leave them.

When we are in Mendi we never
hear of such a thing as men taken away
and carried to Cuba, and then return back
home again. The first thing we tell
them will be that great wind bring
us back. We tell them all about
Merica. We tell them about God
and how Jesus Christ, his only beloved
Son, came to down to die for us, and we
tell them to believe, for these your sons
were lost before now. We want you
to give your children to us, give
to the teachers to teach them
to pray, and not to pray to any
thing but God.

Some wicked people here
laugh at all our Committee
for spending so much on Mendi
people. They say we are like dogs
without any home. But if you will
send us home, you will see whether we
be dogs or not. O please let us go
to the Africa. We want to see no more
snow. We no say this place no good,
but we afraid of cold. Cold catch us all
the time.

        With becoming respect &c.,
        MR. CINQUE

SCRIPTURE

The schooner to hell is a cold long
ride, the wind a doctor rapping

your chest, touching your hair
marking it *unusual, warm lamb's*

wool. You shall travel
west, heading into that bed

the sun drops into after another day
of waking cousins caught in chill

oceans. Once there, you won't
find drums, hell has no percussion

to speak of,—here you can only beat
your belly, its sound growing

thin, thinner. Hell is all
coughs, professors saying *bless*

you and writing it down,—you'll
learn the line, the cut, promises

of freedom. You'll wait, counting
voices, sleep, Bible verses. Let all

the hearers of God's word row
forth, bowing, into the world.

November 8, 1841

To the Hon. John Quincy Adams:

Most Respected Sir,—the Mendi people will never
forget your defence of their rights before the Great

Court of Washington. They feel that they owe
to you, in a large measure, their delivery from evil

hands. They will pray for you as long as you live
Mr. Adams. They never forget you. We are about

to go home, to Africa, we reach Mendi very quick,
then tell the people of your kindness. Good

missionary will go with us. We will take black
Bibles in our mouths,—it has been a precious book

in prison, in writing you, in fire, and we love
to read it now we are free. Mr. Adams we want

to make you a present of a beautiful
Bible. Please accept it, and when you look

at it, remember your grateful clients. We read
in this holy book:—*If it had not been the Lord*

upon our backs when men rose up against us,
then they had swallowed us up quick. Blesséd

be the Lord, who has not given us a prey
to their teeth. Our soul is escaped as a bird

out of the fowler's snare,—the snare is broken
and we soar into the gate and airs of Heaven.

> *For the Mendi people,*
> Cinque
> Kinna
> Kale

SERMON

Heaven has to be this
hot shady place where
folks drink from sky

where we *Preach*
now flood with the hint
of rain where no one

crosses *All right* rivers
of hounds & the thirsty
sip from wells full

of flowers & fallen men
where no man owns
any thing or you or your

mama where some *Praise*
the Lord people starve some
don't but no body thins no

one else where it ain't all gold
harps but nothing swims
a slave *A-men*

GENTLEMAN

at sea, near Sierra Leone

January 13, 1842

Dearest Tappan—this Captain good—
no touch Mende people. We have seen
great water—no danger fell upon
us. I tell you to make letters
for those who no touch us. All
Mende people glad for white men

you give to go with us. Mister
Steele—he left ship to find place. He stop
in Tucker's town—who drink rum all
the time—who is a drunkard. Who like
money better than his own soul. He
tell us the ground costs six hundred

bars—Steele would not give so much.
All the rest of Mende left ship to find
their parents. I think that they will
come again. If they no come, I think
God will punish them forever—one
day. You see we are ten now to stay

behind Steele, and three girls. We will
work wood, we will farm and cut
for him every day. You no feel
bad for that—dear friend—some
Mende men will take care
of your mission. Soon I catch

Sierra Leone—my country—make
home—and take care of white
man. Oh, dear Mister Tappan
how I feel for these wondrous
things! I cannot write so true
because the ship rolls. Pray—

Jesus will hear you—if I never
see you in this world—send word
from the next and the new—

GEORGE BROWN (FU-LI)

No. 1.

(1.)Sing-gbe,[**Cin-gue,**](generally spelt *Cinquez*)was born in Ma-ni, in Dzho-poa, *i. e.* in *the open land*, in the Men-di country. The distance from Mani to Lomboko, he says, is ten suns, or days. His mother is dead, and he lived with his father. He has a wife and three children, one son and two daughters. His son's name is *Ge-waw*, (God.) His king, Ka-lum-bo, lived at Kaw-men-di, a large town in the Mendi country. He is a planter of rice, and never owned or sold slaves. He was seized by four men, when traveling in the road, and his right hand tied to his neck. Ma-ya-gi-la-lo sold him to Ba-ma-dzha, son of Shaka, king of Gen-du-ma, in the Vai country. Bamadzha carried him to Lomboko and sold him to a Spaniard. He was with Mayagilalo three nights; with Bamadzha one month, and at Lomboko two months. He had heard of Pedro Blanco, who lived at Te-i-lu, near Lomboko.＊

from **WITNESS**

☛ *A LIBRETTO*

I was not in safety, neither had I rest, neither was I quiet; yet trouble came.

{ JOB 3:26 }

CHOIR (EVENING)

Sang.
Sang against the storm

and through.
Sang the warm rain.

And the cold.
And our voices growing

hoarse with wind.

No talk
of heaven—

though we learnt that
too up-on the ocean.

Blood that isn't kin.

No supper
to sang for. Nothing

but ration. Heaven
ain't the end—

Heaven begins
the steady lifting.

Things I don't have
no word for——

bones lining the ocean floor.

Hush, child.
The rain. My voice all

I carried.

HOMILY

I have been wandered wild over this world
not by choice:—force

found me in my village,
or in sleep, walking the low
lovely huts, my children's voices——

I have been called
from these things to this
world,—never was new

to me—the birds still
sing—the sun—my heart
in the cage of my chest

crying out like a parrot.
I learnt their talk. Caught
and given no more sky, I fought

as any would. The wood
of the slaver against my back
became my back—the bow

and stern of it, the slow
slow sailing.
               Who recalls, if at the prow,
I met a mermaid's welcome?

My wife far and *frozen*—a word
I would not have known
if not for you—who would

guess of mist made
cold? Tho I had heard tell
of Death, I never knew

its stillness could, in cold, have no smell.

The living thing I loved. Stood
and breathed in. Breathed.
They came, the breaths, often

in home's hills,—they came not at all
in that hold, crouched cramped
cattled—Death came for us

among the moaning the rattling,
the men ghosting, wails
of the women, our children quiet . . .

No child should ever say
such quiet. Be loud!
Death there like a sweetness:—

a hum, a milk song each child
grew hush for.

We spoke with hands we did
not have. Our arms not ours,—
to bear and to bury was all

they'd become. The young ones,—
who would no longer
grow one day older—the waves part for

and the squid find. The arms
of the deep—the many
many hands—rock them

into sleep.

All night we sang
not of Death,—the cut
down tree—but of that

fruit you call *free*.

CREDO.

I believe the body——

The body of beggars
& saints—are same—

I have seen
—by my hand—
a man bleed

& be not buried
except by sea——

I believe

I believe in the sound
the soul makes

No rites we were
offered at all—just
dumped—dogs—

O how they despaired us—

Thot us scraps—scars——

I believe in skin

I believe in its span
& its shrill
sanctuary——

CHOIR (TWILIGHT)

And mercy.

And affliction.

And the journey.
The rain.

Not the world—
the water

weighting down
our clothes.

Not the sea.

Nor the chains.

Nor the ocean
unending.

Nor the end.
No——

The sound of someone
sanging in the night.

And beyond.

And the sparrow
high above us.

What my soul
said to me———

And the ten thousand.

And the years. And a time to gather
stones together.

And the dark
that is itself
a light.

WORKSONG

They'd work us till
the work fell

right out of us—
in jail—Colonel

gave us
hoe & axe—

would have us hack
from sun to sun—

A heap see & few know
A heap start & damn few go—

we caught on
how to catch wind—

easier not to hack
but rock

dead easy—we'd make
verses—versions

to ease the tension—

wishing ourselves east—
making it—we'd just jack

& call out
them river songs

keeping time—
I ain't no Christian

I never been baptized
Take me out the bottom

Lawd
Before the water rise—

Worked our tails off
long that river's edge—

I'd start—buttcut
a tree & the men

followed me—sang
instead of running

our mouths, or away—
we'd make a day that way—

Go on down old hannah
Don't you rise no more

If you rise in the mornin
Lawd Lawd

Bring judgement sure—
Colonel was cruel

not unusual—his punish
meant he'd get the bat

& lick you—
as the leather'd leave

the hide'd leave with it
so you couldn't lie

back in your cell—
Colonel will you spare me

Just one more day
Count of my row so heavy

My knees startin to sway—
by the end our backs

would bow—still
we'd sing those trees

or weeds—never miss
a beat—never pull-do

or chop off a toe—
Look up at old hannah

She's a-turning red
Look at my old partner

He's half most dead—
Colonel worked folks

still in the underworld—
there wasn't no sick—he think

a man a mule—

Wake up O dead man
Help me carry my row

Old partner stare at hannah—
Say he can't go no mo—

We kept up that rhythm—
rolling—from sun to sun—

we kept the Colonel pacified—
like a child—rocked

& sang down all them trees
before we even knowed—

If I had you rider
Where you done got me

I'd wake up some bright morning
And I would set you free

CHOIR (DUSK)

Such sailing——
a wind carrying

us where.
The day steers east

toward the rising

and at night we drift
against the day.

Make it plain—

Mornings I miss
my life the most—

All night I'm back
among the living—

what may be
my dead

since I've left—
stolen west—

Mornings I miss
my life———

my beloved's hands,
our children near-grown.

Or, grown
no more.

Morning's a thin bed—

if, can call this cold
cell, straw floor, a bed.

Here, men dissect
the night sky like the dead

& map our heads
with the dark & stars.

My stomach like
they say of leaves—
turning.

Some nights I want
to walk home cross
wide water

Others only to join
the shifting choir

of the closest river.

CATECHISM

Soiled-on men, the dying children, the women
folded upon each other—this, what
some call a world, really is

upside down. Savaged, ravaged
by the cannibal eyes of the cruel—
by those who would call themselves

master or *señor* or *Christian*
or all three—their eating eyes—
their *thou shalt not*

Then they turn us chattel, our cries

a tongue that can be cut out
our heads. Was. (It flopped
on deck a pink snake

headless.) Once
I planted,—a farmer who knelt
to sweet soil and coaxed

the crops from it
who watched and shepherded the rice
who drew out the white
    from the husks

I who have boiled
and fried, who have fed my family
with blesséd grain brought from the mouths
    of gods I bent to also

I who have knelt to the earth
—and knew nothing of the *blood*—

Now am washed in your Lord Lamb's Red.

Your light (Lawd) has lifted
me up—has led me—

when lost at sea it sent
me homeward—some nights
it sent me fog—
some, such stars.

Now in this cold, this cell—steel
on my ankles—manacles—

in this chill country, the light
I dreamt:—
some seeps down, past the windows
and skeleton keyholes

into my waiting mouth.
I praise

Thee, the light and the warmth both.

Sometime I was sent storms
—or we—the black ivory
the live, long-tooth memory

of being stole—and sick—
We was wretchéd
and knew it

We prayed (at times) the ship
would wreck
save us from all this

Then the lightning, the fires
in sky while
the storm still swam around us

with the sharks. And us—we—
stood inside the storm
like the whale

The well carried the ill
till none was well

And ill held the ill awhile

And the ill held on until
into our palm—mine—
(O why Lawd)

You delivered the nail—
the small steel
the forged belief

that would free us—pry
open our chains—as pearls

stole from the shimmery,
stubborn, lockjaw lips

of our oyster-firm foothold faith.

Lawd, do not let me
among the damnéd be

Pull me apart
from those You leave

When I split this
skin, my soul

lead me
like the sheep
among lions

and there in peace lie.

Where I live
are lions.

Where I lived
lions also did.

Where I live there
are no sheep, only meat
of goats here says
is no good

I don't
want to be left
O God, among the goats

But to be brought
before Your beautiful
slaughter:—

Your hand high
above the altar

raised, the dagger

Then down, bloodied,
lambed, a lantern
small, seaworthy,

into Your large lighthouse light.

COVENANT

    As after rain
I am *a* man
drencht, wrung

free from Faith,
from you, Lawd——

    Drowned, as did
BRO. FOONE who swam out,
strong, into the pond
and sank himself

—his heart a *stone*—

   They drug him
from the lake like a thing
swallowed—

   limp as a garment
with no body in it——

I too have seen
fish swim free
from the hands & nets

 seen the many
(fishes) made from the few—

     By a dance for the old
    gods, we buried him

   —so too, will I
follow, Lawd—
my face among the
shallows

all bone and shadow——

DEVOTIONAL

   Among the grey
New England cemeteries
we might yet
be buried in,—

   Among the Glory
that is Thine—
this and this and
these—

We are boarded
borne—the cold
creeps our bones
—stays—

But we bide,
my Lawd, as you have
said—we should—
    our time

    So shall
the meek inherit

We are handed down
like wisdom, or drunkenness,
by men in wigs

    Hear me O Lawd—

We are not soon
we are
we are not
soon for this world
    some know as New,—

By my Maker
I must rise—must—
and soon—and will

    have flown from this
from this west—

        No more, no more,
        No more auc-tion block
        for me—

We hide our wings
—wishes—like a skeleton
key—on our knees

knowing you will
(soon) spirit us
into æther:—

East:—I will,
to all, tell
of Easter,—how Son

of God three days
and could not sleep
did not,—

                    Went
                on the Way
                —upward—

    Go then:

Draw nigh for
the Kingdom
    is our hand:—
palms grown
with prayer,—tired—

fingers outstretched
begging,—a bounty
and we will be

    on our way—the path
the righteous
take is long

Third day the rock
rolled back,—revealed—

    Lawd I tire
    of this cold——

Send word
—I beg of thee—
and I will bid

    fare well—

No more peck of corn for me

No more driver's lash for me

No more pint of salt &c.——

    I bide
and bite this tongue,—

chomping the bit
I know of the Word

    I am horseman
to the Lawd,—

        And lead us not—

    And from this valley
Merica,—from the shadow—
what say you?

    From Greenland's I-cy
mountain-tops
Shall we whose souls
are lighted &c.——

From this I shall
have flown—seen no more
snow—*soon*—

CHOIR (DARK)

I asked for God
& got only faith

I asked for death
Got only disease

I asked for faith
& was given rain

I asked for belief
& got only belief

I asked for water
Got salt & sea

I asked for home
& got only a place

nowhere near here

I asked to return
to what was gone

& was given heaven

I prayed for heaven
& got only stars

I asked for wine
Got only blood

I asked for blood
& got only God

washing stained hands

I asked for miles
& got these feet

making their way
cross the wide & deep

I begged for rest——
& got only sleep.

ANOINTING

Days I wish I were water
& could walk
then across the Greater

Greying Sea & lay my head
down beside her,
my wife & love. Instead,

I am like the *ice*
brought us
that first winter

here—between sermons
& our hands
it burned

like coal, giving us a feel
for what you call *hell*—
watched it puddle

in my hands
& cell. Gone.
Home is this thirst

for what's there
no longer—
cool heaven

our steady friend.

SECOND ECLECTIC READER.

Progressive Reading & Spelling

LANGUAGE LESSONS.

CONCERT PHONIC DRILL.

strike	might	i rons	suc cess
a right	gazing	climb	stum'ble

EXERCISE.
Drive the nail aright, boys,
  Hit it on the head,
Strike with all your might, boy
  While the irons read.

When you ve work to do, boys,
  Do it with a will,
They who reach the top, boys,
  First must climb the hill.

Standing at the foot, boys,
    Gazing at the sky,
How can you get up, boys,
    If you never try?

nail, you've, succeed, aright,
reach, might, though, climb,
iron.

EXERCISE.
1. Blue-eyes took her_____.
   with her wherever she_____

2. She was_____of_____, for that
   was the doll's_____.

3. I think_____was a_____
   good_____.

3. Don't you_____she had a
   _____doll_____morning?

WORDS TO BE SPELLED:
whose, fair, niece, need,
beads, ladies, dollars, much,
curls, where, yonder, every,
ribbon, laid, said, money,
story, head, sale, buy.

★

SLATE WORK.
This is Mary's reading book.
Is this Mary's reading book?

Apples are good to eat.
We must study our lessons.

I am going home to-night.

EPIPHANY.

Are there slaves in heaven?

Being here
I've learnt the body

is a brute
who keeps

the soul a slave
in its unbroken cage—

where it paces, parades
forth & forth

hoping—to be fed—

or to learn mercy
as the body

that near abandons it—
the soul kept

in rags, hungry
as fate. Forward

is all the soul
knows—is how

it is called—
how it burns

for freedom,
articulate as a limb.

Bides its time. Prays
it is not sold—

Only death
manumits us—

Smaller than
a wish, & less

sure, the soul
rises, takes up arms

against the hounds—
of heaven—

ASH WEDNESDAY.

Once I thought everything
has a soul

Then I learnt only
the fool fears the tree—

It is empty—

So too the wind
that sends it which

way & that—

Now I know God
is such a wind

from which we
are rent—

The heavens take
the tree

from the tree—
leaf by leaf—

Being gone, taken,
is what means Heaven—

It is full—of wings—

A music of what
is missing

since nothing
but men have souls

tho, it appears,
not many.

CHOIR (MORNING)

*May the river
remember you.*

May the road
be your only cross.

May you rise.

May your son
not the silence,
take your hand.

May the lost.

May the mountain
move to meet you

May the climb
be quick.

May the mountain.

May the sea shut
at last its door

May the moon.

May the ash,
not the snow.

May the ground
swallow you whole,
and the sun.

May the last
be the first.

May the lost.

May the stars
for once be still.

Forget heaven——

May you wake
again with the rain.

RAPTURE

OCCASIONAL POEMS

{ 2009–2013 }

WEDDING SONG

for Aaron & Niesha

Help me sing my sorrows
    into smallness.

Help me—

Turn me
    into thee.

I shelter
    & summon you.

I will dance
    you also.

I have only these two lives
    to meet you in.

This hand.

How long then.

This ring.

Answer anything—

Husband me
    into heaven.

Belief our bouquet—

Wedding not what
    we say, but do.

Almost there.

We'll wife our way—

Meet me in the middle
of the air.

26 SEPTEMBER 2009

ANTHEM

Life is a near
death experience.

You can go
to hell, I'm goin

to Texas. It costs
more than a penny

to make a penny.
A dollar for your

thoughts, & a dream.
People have to *breathe*

where they live.
A town big

as her hair.
Aren't there more

worlds than three?
Texas is finally

free, but not its lunch.
Cleave can mean

to sunder
or to meet. The threat

must be imminent.
Look & see—

the daffodils, the rain sage
upright, the high

desert, fire warnings,
the scorched trees. Cloven,

clove, clave, cleavage,
cleft. Every day's

a lottery. Hoods,
blood. The death

of the Canadian penny
means we all may need

to round up. Leaves,
left. Bereave,

bereft.

30 MARCH 2012

WHOLE HOG

i.m. Jake Adam York

It is heavy,
a hog, you need
to stay

up all night, nursing
the fire like a beer—
or rise early

like we did, that first time
you taught me how
to drag December

awake into flame,
lighting pecan
& hickory passed

between cinder block
& ash. Do you dig
a pit? No—

we build one
last house
for the huge sow

who we know
rooted & ranged
the given ground.

Head on, scrubbed, split,
the pig's skin
crackles, a communion

of it—no spit,
just shoveling coals
like a locomotive

engineer, boilerman,
rounder—
Casey Jones

*mounted to his cabin
& he took his farewell
trip to the promised land—*

the smoke everywhere
like a prayer, clinging
your clothes for days

we do not wish
to wash away. To share
the weight, to wear it—

to honor the creature
by devouring it
whole—we know she

would return
the favor. *He looked
at his watch*

*& his watch
was slow.* Steam rises sweet
among the maples

& bamboo. How
do you know
it is done? The hog

will tell you.

CHRISTMAS EVE DAY 2012

BLUISH

i.m. Lucille Clifton
1936–2010

Nothing on.
       Only sequels now
you'll never see—

though maybe that's lucky—
       or men wearing blades
on their feet, thin

as the ice they race
       across. Once,
among your boxes, my hands

lifted most all
       you wrote—saving
what you saved—sifting

while you fed letters
       to the black
trash bag. We all

need rescue—
       I learnt that from you—
your words

a life preserver
       ringing you—
no halo. How

already I miss you.
       No word
yet on the late news—

I should have known
        only you
tonight would send south

such deep, bluish snow.

*

Out of nowhere, over-
        night, my ceiling stained.
The fragments that fall.

The dogs & their bones
        & barks busy the hall.
In the kitchen glasses break

barely touched.
        What's the rush?
Sleeping light, the sounds

I now know
        are only my own.
It's all too much—

the floorboards complain
        when touched,
loud as my drunken

downstairs neighbor
        shouting over
his arguing TV. Above,

I've grown silent
        as wine. Careful
as the broken glass

I pick up slowly so's
        not to cut. My ceiling a dark
brown eye—water somewhere

enters, divining.

*

Like a syringe
        the thermometers empty,
words turn to mercury—

break & leak.
        We believe in our
breath because

cold now, we can see it.
        What to
say now? A truck

beep-beep-beeps
        backing up, covered
in salt & dirt pleading

WASH ME.
        These are days to ignore
whatever covers us, making sure

winter won't win.
        Green beneath
the snow drifts. My hands

numb writing this.

*

If you can, fall.
        If you can't, call
& I'll come. I'll be the one

with the red
        handkerchief spilling
from my hand.

This world I've found
        is a farm
fresh egg—brown,

or green, bluish—
        small & not all
it's cracked up

to be. You knew this
        world blooms
its twin yolks

into a clear bowl—
        once opened
it must

become something else.

*

Winter, even here.
        For you I won't
observe no moment

of silence, my tongue
        a polite
riot, a flock

of teeth like frost
        spidering the panes.
This voice, yours, holds

the sound of plenty ice
        thawing all
at once. The twang

of things shouted
        lowercase. Today,
walking without

a hat, looking to find
        where the cold
comes from, I saw

instead this rebuttal
        scrawled along
a wall: *Nope.*

The sound of snow—slipping
        from the brown embrace
of the trees—meets

the hush below.

ELEGY FOR HEANEY

i.m. Seamus Heaney 1939–2013

Your voice in my ear
like the sea. I heard
your last words—
in Latin no less—

were *Do not fear.*
(I keep wanting
to write *are.*)
I hear *Noli timere*

everywhere—eyes, nose,
summoned lungs.
You knew many
untied tongues—

even some dead ones—
that you bid sing.
What's left now
to praise? Everything.

＊

In your class we began
with the Seven Stages
of Man, or Woman, or even
us students, green,

yet that was the point—
Write a poem of *infans,*
you said. *Without speech*
it means & mine the next week

had a slave child, hid,
who didn't know just how
old he was. It wasn't
bad, the poem, as might be—

me eighteen—& I still recall
not exactly what you said
but how it sent me
away thinking maybe

one day, I too,
might speak. What
we think we don't
always thank

but you strove to—
a nod, a lean,
sideburns blazing. Even
your ears had wings.

＊

*All my favorite poets
are dead*, I said,
meaning you
& her & him

whom I was lucky
I once knew. And still
maybe I do—
though like most

almost orphans,
I know how
alone we all
must learn to sing.

This the way
the world begins—
with a word,
with a light

hand, like you had,
a head sometime
heavy & some verb
& verve to write—

a ship to right.
On your back you sailed.
Across this earth to which
our feet are nailed.

SEPTEMBER 2013

A SHORT BLESSING
FOR A LONG MARRIAGE

for Cole & Julie

Before we
had children, we thought

we understood
the world—now that

I do
I understand

the earth. Today
is another birth.

21 SEPTEMBER 2013

THERE IS A LIGHT
THAT NEVER GOES OUT

Don't dream it's over you don't
know what's it's like it's like that
& that's the way it be near me be near
close to you crazy for you got the look
what you done done a do run run
run away run away she was lying
in the grass & she was it something
I said I know what boys like a prayer
a virgin girls just wanna boys
don't cry don't don't you
want me don't fall on me O
what a feelin' more than keep
feeling fascination *hush hush*
voices carry too shy too shy close
to me & you don't you
forget about hold me now don't try
to live your life in one day it's my
life nobody walks in LA woman
every breath you take you take
my breath away there's always
something in the water
does not compute no new
tale to tell me if you still care
computer love went to her house
to bust a move & had to leave
real early tell me tell me
how to be you & me when I'm alone
in my room sometimes I stare at where
are you calling from call me
tell me fall on me let me be your time
will reveal won't give me time I'll
stop the world shut your mouth
on mine I can't I can't I can't
stand losing cause this

is thriller thriller night fine
young pretty young thing is ooh
I like it sends chills up you gots
to chill party up you got to let
me know nobody loves you I am
only human & need you back
in love again bring on
the dancing let's dance let's
stay together & dance this mess
around dance dance dance
see how we are family I got
all I need to get by your side
to side back & forth word up for
the down stroke me everybody
wants you let's go crazy let's pretend
we're married let's wait awhile
again spin me right round baby
I'm a star under the milky way
tonight.

2013

RAPTURE

I want to be awake
when the world ends.
I want to be my friend

who rose to an empty
house, even his grandmother
& her worn cross gone

& thought it was the rapture,
that he hadn't crossed over.
Let me rip my shirt

as he did & tear into the street
hollering. Let me hear
only my blood beat this morning

in the rain before the dawn—
no one on the line.
Later, when they return,

let those I love who left
have only gone to the store,
running errands, this errant

unebbing life. After,
let what I've torn—
the myself I mourn—

be mended & start
over, like a scar,
or star.

from

BOOK *of* HOURS

———————————

BEREAVEMENT

Behind his house, my father's dogs
sleep in kennels, beautiful,
he built just for them.

They do not bark.
Do they know he is dead?
They wag their tails

& head. They beg
& are fed.
Their grief is colossal

& forgetful.
Each day they wake
seeking his voice,

their names.
By dusk they seem
to unremember everything—

to them even hunger
is a game. For that, I envy.
For that, I cannot bear to watch them

pacing their cage. I try to remember
they love best confined space
to feel safe. Each day

a saint comes by to feed the pair
& I draw closer
the shades.

I've begun to think of them
as my father's other sons,
as kin. Brothers-in-paw.

My eyes each day thaw.
One day the water cuts off.
Then back on.

They are outside dogs—
which is to say, healthy
& victorious, purposeful

& one giant muscle
like the heart. Dad taught
them not to bark, to point

out their prey. To stay.
Were they there that day?
They call me

like witnesses & will not say.
I ask for their care
& their carelessness—

wish of them forgiveness.
I must give them away.
I must find for them homes,

sleep restless in his.
All night I expect they pace
as I do, each dog like an eye

roaming with the dead
beneath an unlocked lid.

ACT NOW & SAVE

It's a wonder the world
keeps its whirling—

How I've waited
without a word—

Staring where
the sun's no longer—

You gone
into ether, wherever

You want
to call it. Soon

Sun won't fight
off the cold

But today warm
even in the rain.

Whatever the well
you want me

To fall down I will—

Meet me by the deepest
part of the river

And we'll drown together
wading out past

All care, beyond even
the shore's hollers.

EFFECTS

It was a ghost
      town, a town
not of the dead

but the deserted—
      once thriving—a hospital
named not for a saint

nor Women & Children—
      whoever's first—but for the city
where you'd been flown

for now. The help desk
      was no help. You
were somewhere

else, already your body lost
      in the basement dark,
where, if you had eyes

left, they soon would adjust
      & you could see.
The last to see you

being helped
      to breathe
was your friend the Judge

I asked over the phone
      to look in on you
in your next-

to-last room, to make sure
      the rehearsed nurse
told the truth. Your brain

dead, body a machine—
       It's bad,
he said, acting

as my eyes. Yours
       I soon would give—
flown here to retrieve

your effects
       from a chilly teller,
this banker of bodies.

Well below
       in the morgue, the walls
of the dead in their safe

deposit boxes—
       your wallet handed back
signed for, unspent. What

was left. The lobby
       like a cathedral bombed
but whose rose

window still shone—
       me a prisoner released
too early, on furlough,

with nowheres
       to go. Outside
strangely spring

but cold—on break,
       nurses in their abstract
expressionist shirts

huddled & shared
        cigarettes, exhaling
thick halos of smoke.

RUE

Strange how you keep on
   dying—not once
then over

& done with—or for—
   if not every day
anymore, each morning

a sabbath of sundering,
   then hours still arrive
I realize nothing

can beg you back—
   nor return to us days
without harm, heaven

only an idea. Hell not yet
   that week
I couldn't bear to sleep

in your half-life house
   & my future
wife & I stayed

at the Worst
   Western, the phone
ringing early, & late,

too late. I'd wake

& you'd be there, gone—
   retreating
to the bleak bathroom

& its heat lamp, perched
        on the edge
of the empty tub, I'd try

not to write.
        How terrible
to have to pick up

the pen, helpless
        to it, your death
not yet

a habit & try to say
        something other than
never, or *hereafter*,

to praise among the tile—
        not your dying—
but having

been alive. The pale bathroom

whose light burnt on, red
        as a darkroom,
ticking down—

your eulogy dashed out
        among the tiny
broken soap, each day

shrinking, slivered
        in our hands. Come late
afternoon, the distant, wet slaps

of children poolside
      crying out
in laughter—their muffled

watery shrieks echoing after.

MERCY

On line for the plane
a woman carried her heart
on her lap & I thought

could it be yours
she held tight? It wasn't
her heart yet

of course, was her future
heart, I guess, soon
inside her beating

after being dead
on the table, a minute
or two, during surgery

in a hospital named Mercy.
For now, wheeled
alongside her, her almost

heart sat labeled
& tucked in its red chest
of ice. I thought

I could be her
holding you, hoping
there was enough life left in you

to help me
again breathe.
I knew full well

you were not there,
father, that it was your liver
lifted out of you

& set like a bloody stone
inside somebody
else to save. After being

checked for danger, just
beyond the glass doors,
I watched

a farmer father
& mother send off
their plaid son

the first time he'd flown,
everyone wiping their eyes
& waving.

GRIEF

In the night I brush
my teeth with a razor

CHARITY

So many socks.

After the pair
the undertaker asks for
(I picture them black

beneath the fold
in your open casket,
your toes still cold)

what else to do.
Body bags
of old suits, shirts

still pressed, long
johns, the unworn,
unwashed wreckage

of your closet, too many
coats to keep, though I will save
so many. How can I

give away the last
of your scent? And still,
father, you have errands,

errant dry cleaning to pick up—
yellow tags whose ghostly
carbon tells a story

where to look. One
place closed
for good, the tag old.

One place with none
of your clothes,
just stares as if no one

ever dies, as if you
are naked somewhere,
& I suppose you are.

Nothing here.
The last place knows exactly
what I mean, brings me shirts

hanging like a head.
Starched collars
your beard had worn.

One man saying sorry, older lady
in the back saying how funny
you were, how you joked

with her weekly. *Sorry*—
& a fellow black man hands
your clothes back for free,

don't worry. I've learned death
has few kindnesses left.
Such is charity—so rare

& so rarely free—
that on the way back
to your emptying house

I weep. Then drive
everything, swaying,
straight to Goodwill—

open late—to live on
another body
& day.

WINTERING

I am no longer ashamed
how for weeks, after, I wanted
to be dead—not to die,

mind you, or do
myself in—but to be there
already, walking amongst

all those I'd lost, to join
the throng singing,
if that's what there is—

or the nothing, the gnawing—
So be it. I wished
to be warm—& worn—

like the quilt my grandmother
must have made, one side
a patchwork of color—

blues, green like the underside
of a leaf—the other
an old pattern of the dolls

of the world, never cut out
but sewn whole—if the world
were Scotsmen & sailors

in traditional uniforms.
Mourning, I've learned, is just
a moment, many,

grief the long betrothal
beyond. Grief what
we wed, ringing us—

heirloom brought
from my father's hot house—
the quilt heavy tonight

at the foot of my marriage bed,
its weight months of needling
& thread. Each straightish,

pale, uneven stitch
like the white hairs I earned
all that hollowed year—pull one

& ten more will come,
wearing white, to its funeral—
each a mourner, a winter,

gathering ash at my temple.

PITY

The cookies his neighbors brought by
    didn't taste like pity—

at my father's house
    for the first time, after, the locks

broken into, now new, when cross
    the street comes

a neighbor, cookies shrouded
    in tinfoil, a plate

I need not return.
    How long had the pair

kept vigil out the window
    for someone to set foot here

so they might make their offering?
    Had they begun baking

soon as they heard, knowing
    full well the dead

& those closest to them
    grow hungry?

Like bread
    the body rising.

Inside, his house filled
    with what killed him—

a dozen turkey decoys deflating,
    bright empty shells.

Another kind soul had taped a tarp
     over his open sunroof top.

Disarray, the rest. Who knows
     what goes where? After

all, it is dirt we return to—or fire
     we devour—the pool

we once swam out back
     now drained, flooding the street

in mock calamity—no longer
     the filter sucking

its lower lip & teeth
     like a child trying

hard not to weep.

CODICIL

May God or whoever else
    spare you

the arms of bereavement
    specialists—

grant mercy from the Team
    dedicated to your transition

in this difficult time
    yet who won't tell you

a thing & know far less.
    Those innocent, interminable,

polite, unreachable
    voices over the phone—

do not suffer those—
    they are unlike death

who does not ask
    or give one whit

for your death certificate
    they need

duplicates of.
    No, originals.

No, now three letters
    of testamentary

six pounds of flesh—
    whatever's left.

Hell is not a live
    voice—just listen

to the complete menu
    as our options have changed.

Press One
    for Purgatory.

Two for shame.
    Three to get ready

Four for blame.
    Five years

of phone calls to sort
    your death out—

& one day, the avenging angel
    of telemarketing leaves

a message not asking
    after you, but acting

as if you & she
    had spoken, today—

*Paul, just wanted
    to get back to you*

about the cruise.

My response
    was what the afterlife

must be like—
    quick, mean, a piece

of my mind & passing
   along no peace—

just righteousness—if ever
   she called back

I said, *I'd kill her*—
   & not with kindness

as does the phone.
   Better to go it alone.

ANNIVERSARY

The day will come

when you'll be dead longer
than alive—thankfully

not soon.
There are of course years

long before, without you
breathing—and your years

without me even
an idea. Then there are those

infant months, when I knew
your voice, your bearded

face, not your name—
at least to speak

it aloud. And in the night,
father, I cried out

and in the day—
like now.

EXPECTING

Grave, my wife lies back, hands cross
her chest, while the doctor searches early
for your heartbeat, peach pit, unripe

plum—pulls out the world's worst
boombox, a Mr. Microphone, to broadcast
your mother's lifting belly.

The whoosh and bellows of mama's body
and beneath it: nothing. Beneath
the slow stutter of her heart: nothing.

The doctor trying again to find you, fragile
fern, snowflake. Nothing.
After, my wife will say, in fear,

impatient, she went beyond her body,
this tiny room, into the ether—
for now, we spelunk for you one last time

lost canary, miner of coal
and chalk, lungs not yet black—
I hold my wife's feet to keep her here—

and me—trying not to dive starboard
to seek you in the dark water. And there
it is: faint, an echo, faster and further

away than mother's, all beat box
and fuzzy feedback. You are like hearing
hip-hop for the first time—power

hijacked from a lamppost—all promise.
You couldn't sound better, break-
dancer, my favorite song bumping

from a passing car. You've snuck
into the club underage and stayed!
Only later, much, will your mother

begin to believe your drumming
in the distance—our Kansas City
and Congo Square, this jazz band

vamping on inside her.

STARTING TO SHOW

She sleeps on the side
her heart is on—

sleeps facing the sun
that juts through our window

earlier and earlier. In the belly
of the sky the sun kicks

and cries. My wife
has begun to wear the huge

clothes of inmates, smuggling you
inside her—son

or daughter. I bring her
crackers and water.

Wardens of each other,
in the precincts

of unsteady sleep, we drift
off curled

like you are, listening
to the night breathe.

FIRST KICK

More like
a flicker, a far-
off flutter

beneath my
broad hand—
then, two

weeks later,
a nudge, a knee
as you elbow

round inside—
acrobat, apple
of our eye

we can't
yet see. You seed
my mind

with nicknames,
Buddy. Junior,
you drift

like an astronaut
tethered silver
to the mothership.

You are even better
than fruit
floating in Jell-O!

We cannot wait
to welcome you
with ticker tape—

no slap—
when at last you arrive
and find life

on our puny planet.

DELIVERY

I believe birth a lengthy process
    meant to help us believe
    in the impossible.

I believe the body knows
    more than we do.

I believe pregnancy is meant
    to teach us patience,
    then impatience. To ready
    for what cannot be.

I believe it does not matter
    what I believe.

I believe aches now,
    heartbreak later.

I believe the body is meant
    to emerge from another body,
    to merge with it.

I believe that the body begins
    far outside the skin.

I believe in you mewling my name
    until it is yours,
    then mine again.

I believe that heat can stay
    with us for days,
    that cold is only an instant,
    then always.

CROWNING

Now that knowing means nothing,
now that you are more born
than being, more awake
than awaited, since I've seen
your hair deep inside mother,
a glimpse, grass in late
winter, early spring, watching
your mother's pursed, throbbing,
purpled power, her pushing
you for one whole hour, two,
almost three, almost out,
maybe never, animal smell
and peat, breath and sweat
and mulch-matter, and at once
you descend, or drive, are driven
by mother's body, by her will
and brilliance, by bowel,
by wanting and your hair
peering as if it could see, and I saw
you storming forth,
taproot, your cap of hair half
in, half out, and *wait, hold
it there,* the doctors say, and
she squeezing my hand, her face
full of fire, then groaning your face
out like a flower, blood-bloom,
crocused into air, shoulders
and the long cord still rooting
you to each other, to the other
world, into this afterlife
amongst us living, the cord
I cut like an iris, pulsing,
then you wet against mother's chest
still purple, not blue, not yet
red, no cry,

warming now, now opening
your eyes midnight
blue in the blue black dawn.

COLOSTRUM

We are not born
with tears. Your

first dozen cries
are dry.

It takes some time
for the world to arrive

and salt the eyes.

JAUNDICE

It's hard being
human. This morning yellow

overtook you, a thousand
yolks broken beneath

your skin. Splotches
of red, and you not rousing,

drowsy, listless—your head dips
like a drunk's, or a duck

in a shooting gallery. Wrung,
we ring and bring you to a doctor

whose worried brown face
I try hiding from your mother—

she weeps over your body
mottled, bare, losing weight—

your black, burnt-
looking belly button, even

your feet flushed.
What color

should you be?
Hard to say

my black-eyed
susan, barely born, the flowers

brought by you
and last week's visitors

freshly cut, bowed in water.
Tomorrow maybe

we'll breathe.
For now we worry

the waiting room, watch
the clock wind us—

television showing the anniversary
of September's calamities

that seem worlds away
and yesterday.

You roll to the nursery
to tan under blue light

we pray will bake
the poison out. In fever

your body burns
like a martyr. Pietà,

hothouse hope, you rise up
hours later—lighter

and darker too. The yellow
leaving you. Eyes

still not white
but opening slow. What color

should you be?
After mama nurses

you, I feed you formula
on doctor's orders, color

of buttermilk, eggnog
maybe—saying

wake up, the almost
milk everywhere spilling.

GREENING

It never ends, the bruise
     of being—messy,
untimely, the breath

of newborns uneven, half
     pant, as they find
their rhythm, inexact

as vengeance. Son,
     while you sleep
we watch you like a kettle

learning to whistle.
     Awake, older,
you fumble now

in the most graceful
     way—grateful
to have seen you, on your own

steam, simply eating, slow,
     chewing—this bloom
of being. Almost beautiful

how you flounder, mouth full, bite
     the edges of this world
that doesn't want

a thing but to keep turning
     with, or without you—
with. With. Child, hold fast

I say, to this greening thing
     as it erodes
and spins.

THIRST

What blossoms
    is loss—
last year's ash

fills a tin from the grill
    that fed us all
last summer like a father—

that black belly
    rusty, its grate
you scrape, hopefully not too clean—

the past where
    taste lives,
seasoning—sudden weeds

taller than even
    you dreamed, bending
bare arms to the earth

to yank them out by their hair.
    The hollies finally
given up on—

the dead harder
    to root out than
you'd think, worms

weaving round the dirt
    black, lush, clinging—
the ferns somehow returned,

planted in that heat wave
    last summer, remember, sweat
stinging the eyes, wilting—

now their green
          palms wide open
in offering. The steady

consolation of things
          returning—lilac
and dogwood, sweet woodruff, even

the stones shine
          in the sun. White blooms
soon gone—

soothing thud
          of the neighbor girl playing
catch, catgut kissing leather

or missed, the ball landing soft
          in our yard's
deep grass—*so sorry*

for your loss—only the tulips
          refusing to rise
this spring, stung

by the freezer all winter
          we kept them in.
Like any good son, mine

still tends the dirt, watering
          the bulbs long after
they're done—with his little cup

tries to fill the darkness up.

PIETÀ

I hunted heaven
for him.

No dice.

Too uppity,
it was. Not enough

music, or dark dirt.

I begged the earth empty
of him. Death

believes in us whether
we believe

or not. For a long while
I watch the sound

of a boy bouncing a ball
down the block

take its time
to reach me. Father,

find me when
you want. I'll wait.

RUTH

Every pore mourns.
Not the brain, nor
the chest where bereavement

nests, but the body, whole—
how it burns.
The ache of new bone

being grown.

————————

That summer the faith
of a fever bent me
to my knees. Or flat

on my aching back, shivering
like a tree. I cannot keep anything
down all week. I thrush

& thrash, quarantined, thirst
to know what's happening
among the rooms

of the living.

————————

Bedridden, I can barely see
the clear, glacial lake
where tiger mussels swept upstream

by boat & accident
cut the feet, devouring
everything, like grief,

till there's no more—
which, next year, is what
they'll be—like my father

is already.

—————

Sharper than stone
or woe, the mussels soon
will eat themselves

into extinction—
two summers
later, floating far

from the shore—
you cannot mourn
forever—my infant son will cry

with delight while passed,
kicking, between our
watery hands. For now,

the ashen world without him

—————

has come to live,
unspoken, a sore
along my tongue—

swollen like an adder
whose prey takes weeks
to devour. My skin

on fire, wished
to be shed—or molting,
swallowing stone.

My soon hollow bones.

————————

They shine in me a light.
I lie still,
transported into the white

hum, naked beneath
a shroud, while they sift
& read my blood.

It's mum. No one
can name
what's sought

to undo me this season—
some bug, locust god,
or hex? The dead

crouched on my chest.

————————

Autumn now all
around us, the abscess
slow erodes—

of life there's always
only less.
Even healing

hurts. Our bodies
leave us little
choice—scars

that way are ruthless—
what's mended
stitched stronger

than what gaped

———————

there before. So this
is what
it means to mourn:

the horse pills
I choke back
for weeks—like the food

you must down them with—
are almost more
painful than whatever

they cure.

———————

Lips cracked open
like an egg, half-dead,
all night I toss & churn—

featherless bird
its mother feeds
from her own mouth—

maw of what sustains
that almost
swallows

us whole—
the pain newborn
& ravenous, fledgling,

then flown.

ARBOR DAY

It's supposed to be beautiful tomorrow
should be New England's motto.

Instead it's Shut up & drive.
Or, I never met a lane
I didn't like. Often two at the same time.

Once I watched, while the rest
of us pulled over, someone drive past
then turn left—crash—

into a flashing ambulance.
At least she used
a turn signal.

So when we lost the wanted, not-
yet child, it was supposed to be
nice outside

but wasn't. Inside the baby
we already had cried
to be read to—

my wife listing room to room.
In brisk, unbloomed April
only the crocus have pulled through.

Tomorrow yard waste
pickup resumes, my helpful
neighbor reminds me—I recollect

last fall's late leaves in sacks
mostly torn behind the house
where all winter they sat,

half preserved, half rot.
Our lawn mostly mud, I lug
the damp, heavy bags—

unwieldy as a body given
six months of winter,
or more—& of course,

or luckily, only
one split. The black
leaves spilling their ink

across the still-brown lawn.
By glove & shovel I shove
the loam into another bag—

IDEAL FOR COMPOSTING SELF—
which, on its own, weighted
along the curb, doesn't manage

to stand. The dead leaves
lean there for weeks,
fraying, a reminder of all

we get wrong, & fate—
turns out I was too early—
before men come at dawn one day

& whisk everything away.

MEMORIAL DAY

I wake early to join
     the others dying
of sweat, or breath, trying

to return to the bodies
     we once owned—
slow going on a quick

track. We orbit
     the fake grass, sun
already high enough to burn

the eyes or arms, windmilling
     for all it's worth.
We keep finding ourselves

in each other's way—silent
     we spin, a cavalcade
of future pain. And then,

in the blue beside
     the ring, up springs
a proper parade—

traffic lined up & ashen
     veterans, three left,
bow their heads

while names are read—
     is that a prayer
I can't make out

above the quick trinity
     of rifle fire, smoke
clouding the air?

None flinch.
    We keep pace along
with our shortening shadows,

every ache a wish.

SORROW

The dogs ate what we did
     only days

later. Like angels
     they roam the countryside

belonging to no one.
     And everyone.

We feed them like sorrow
     to keep them at bay

& to make them stay.
     Like heaven we begin

to expect them each day—
     put out a cracked plate

just in case. Like the dead
     they are impossible

to tame.

PILGRIMAGE

Your love,
Two-headed cow
—R.E.M.

We were west of it,
home I mean, and I was trying

near Death Valley
to write a poem called Heaven

and failing. Impossible,
Paradise—

which is why
we keep reaching.

Instead, the desert

we'd soon enter,
windows down, driving, the heat

blowing us drier
than ever, shirt soaked through.

We'd stopped earlier to see
the sheep with two faces

who lived only an hour—

a six-legged steer
and the World's Largest

Prairie Dog. Which wasn't
ever alive, but worth the price.

It was almost autumn—

sturgeon moon
lifting above the mountains

and mesas—even its light
seemed full of heat.

Paradise was promise,
the poem thankfully lost.

All signs read: Here
was fought the battle

no one won.
Thinner then, I believed

in something moving beyond

the wind. What
did I know then

of extinction? It was all
I wrote about.

Envy the dead—
the flowers, their unmade beds.

How well they dress.

Here I was writing a poem
called Heaven

actually about the earth.
It shook beneath us.

Almost there, windmills
rose up

out of the desert,
churning, rowing

the very air
they made power

out of, and for—
an unseen that made them

move, and mean.

GRAVITY

I have tried telling this before—
how the light stabbed its way
out of the clouds, rays
aimed everywhere—
no, it was the earth that day
drawing light out of the sky,
heavy, gravity pulling
the light to rest on its chest,
a ladder leaning—
in the valley north of the City
of Angels, mountains around us,
my passenger a twin, one
half of two, their mother
killed a year
or so before, helicopter
catching a power line—
gone—and I, knowing nothing
then, or too much, said
little, maybe *sorry*
which isn't all
you can say, but mostly—
though I didn't know that then—
and we were fighting
with my warbling tape deck,
no doubt, when we saw it—
tumbling, end
over end across the highway,
a car flipping and spitting up
dust and God knows
what else—midair—
and almost before I could reach
the shoulder, my friend out
across the lanes, racing
to the crumpled car,
to his mother—even then

I knew it was her he hoped
to meet—instead, in the scorched
grass of the median, a spare
or spared shoe, books flapping
their wings, and a man, dazed, somehow
thrown clear—
kneeling. We were not
the first, already some off-duty nurse
or Samaritan beside him, within
seconds, asking
what I should have—*are you*
alright? He held
no answers, no tongue
for where he had just
been, almost stayed, the car turtled
over on its back, its brokenness
that could be
our bodies, not yet
our lives—or his—and my friend
the twin almost there in time,
me slow behind, the last
of the first—scared to see—
looking on in horror
and wonder, clothes tossed
everywhere now no one would wear—
the broken mirrors missing
bodies they once
were conjoined to—
closer than they appear—
a blinding, splintered sky
helpless we soon would turn
and sail off under.

THE MISSION

Back there then I lived
    across the street from a home

for funerals—afternoons
    I'd look out the shades

& think of the graveyard
    behind Emily Dickinson's house—

how death was no
    concept, but soul

after soul she watched pour
    into the cold

New England ground.
    Maybe it was the sun

of the Mission,
    maybe just being

more young, but it was less
    disquiet than comfort

days the street filled with cars
    for a wake—

children played tag
    out front, while the bodies

snuck in the back. The only hint
    of death those clusters

of cars, lights low
    as talk, idling dark

as the secondhand suits
 that fathers, or sons

now orphans, had rescued
 out of closets, praying

they still fit. Most did. Most
 laughed despite

themselves, shook
 hands & grew hungry

out of habit, evening
 coming on, again—

the home's clock, broke
 like a bone, always

read three. Mornings or dead
 of night, I wondered

who slept there & wrote letters
 I later forgot

I sent my father, now find buoyed up
 among the untidy

tide of his belongings.
 He kept everything

but alive. I have come to know
 sorrow's

not noun
 but verb, something

that, unlike living,
 by doing right

you do less of. The sun
       is too bright.

Your eyes
       adjust, become

like the night. Hands
       covering the face—

its numbers dark
       & unmoving, unlike

the cars that fill & start
       to edge out, quiet

cortège, crawling, half dim, till
       I could not see to see—

from **BOOK OF HOURS**

———

The light here leaves you
lonely, fading

as does the dusk
that takes too long

to arrive. By morning
the mountain moving

a bit closer to the sun.

This valley belongs
to no one—

except birds who name
themselves by their songs

in the dawn.
What good

are wishes, if they aren't
used up?

The lamp of your arms.

The brightest
blue beneath the clouds—

We guess
at what's next

unlike the mountain

who knows it
in the bones, a music

too high
to scale.

———————

The burnt,
blurred world

where does it end—

The wind
kicks up the scent

from the stables
where horseshoes hold

not just luck but
beyond. But

weight. But a body

that itself burns,
begs to run.

The gondola quits just
past the clouds.

The telephone poles
tall crosses in the road.

Let us go
each, into the valley—

turn ourselves
& our hairshirts

inside out, let the world
itch—for once—

————

The sun's small fury
feeds me.

Wind dying down.

We delay, & dither,
then are lifted

into it, brightness
all about—

O setting.
O the music

as we soar
is small, yet sating.

What you want—

Nobody, or nothing
fills our short journeying.

Above even the birds,
winging heavenward,

the world is hard
to leave behind

or land against—
must end.

I mean to make it.

Turning slow beneath
our feet,

finding sun, seen
from above,

this world looks
like us—mostly

salt, dark water.

––––––––

You could spend
a lifetime hoping

to mend the moon.

Tonight let's try—
bent to the fallen

needles, the pines, my hands
weaving

& wanting.

The half-moon
of your heart.

The stars are
so far.

Their light even
death does not end,

late arrives—

they bear
up the world

by their strings
& by example.

Shut your eyes.

The mantle
of midnight grown

light along my shoulder.
Each star a stone

in the river of sky—
the Milky Way's bright tide

wringing me awake.

The few fields
  forgive you—

give way to valleys
  inside the mind

that themselves fill
  with wildflowers—

brown-eyed susans
  swaying, saying

something to the bees
  about beginning

about being
  patient & what is

beyond all this—
  it is always the bloom,

that undoing,
  does me in.

The dogwood we planted
  for my son

now dying—

But it is not the autumn
  I mean to mention.

Nor the winter
  that has overcome

the air just today,
    11th November, & because

I can name it, the end,
    I will.

Still, the bent wood

of a chair, indoors, will
    hold you, the small green

leftover from summer
    will raise you up long

as it can, long
    as you don't fight it.

Being means believing,
    if only what we don't

know yet—
    this quiet, coming,

rare & rarer, but still
    there, below

the buzzing, just there,
    opened after

the white of winter's letters.

How to listen
to what's gone—

To moan & learn—

The geese don't
seem to mind

winter anymore—stay
put & graze.

No more their calls
against the dusk.

Nor their arrows
silhouetted against

this tintype sky—

its silver face, once
touched, begins

to fade fingerprint-grey.

Letters
I've never sent.

This life
we're only renting.

Battered the world is—
bartered—

wander over it,
the stars finding

us wanting.

Does the wind wonder
    about us—

the way it blows
    the blossoms down

it must—the birds start
    their bargaining early

before we awaken

& do our own—
    which may

be too late.

The bare beach
    in winter.

Dogs in the distance,
    the frozen whitecaps.

How far could we walk

across that water?
    Gulls like vultures

eddy above.
    Nearer, the hours

are ours to make
    the most of—

or to learn,
    with practice, to relent.

Scars grow
    smaller.

So too, the future—

Rest, I said.
    Remain—

Return,
    begs the wind

circling what won't
    stay put.

———————

Bodies are built
to fail. To fall

& only once
in a while, to rise.

Otherwise, end.

Otherwise, fade
with the light.

Other arms
will lift you up, I know,

carry you crying
to my grave.

The weeds & weather will
sing my name.

Look away.

Let them let me down
without you watching.

Sunflowers.

Their heads seek the sun—
or bend without one

even after cut—
angling in the water

toward what
brightness we borrow.

———————

It's death there
is no cure for—

life the long
disease.

If we're lucky.

Otherwise, short
trip beyond.

And below.

Noon,
growing shadow.

I chase the quiet
round the house.

Soon the sound—

wind wills
its way against

the panes. Welcome
the rain.

Welcome
the moon's squinting

into space.
The trees

bow like priests.

The storm lifts
up the leaves.

Why not sing.

LINER NOTES

Thanks to everyone over the years who read, published, edited, and helped me with these poems, too many individuals to thank all by name. Though I must mention, in order of how long I've known them: my mother, my late father, Dick, Cole, Lizzie, Tasha, Sean, Eileen, Cathy, David, Nicky, Campbell, Matthew, Michael, and my agent Rob for all their editorial suggestions and other support. I'd especially like to thank Deborah Garrison, my editor for every one of these books since *Jelly Roll* and *Ghosts: the remix*. Endless thanks to my dear wife, Kate, who endured, enabled, and inspired these poems.

"Langston Hughes," "Busking," "Farm Team," "Serenade," "Bereavement," "Expecting," "Crowning," and "Rapture" first appeared in *The New Yorker*. Thanks to editors Alice Quinn and Paul Muldoon.

The notes that follow are in the order of their appearance in *Blue Laws*, and appeared in their original book's order.

GLOSSOLALIA (1997)
Written for a catalog, never published, for my friend the artist Ellen Gallagher.

TO REPEL GHOSTS (2001; 2005)
To give a visual idea of Basquiat's hand, SMALL CAPITALS generally indicate painted/drawn text found in his work. Titles often correspond to paintings; the dates following titles apply to the work and are included to indicate a sense of the history of the art and artist. (Dates are *not* the dates of my composition.) Basquiat, in the context of the seeming casualness of his canvases, put it best: "Everything is well stretched even though it looks like it might not be."

As might be expected, a show about Basquiat includes found text and imagery. The following list includes those things not common knowledge or property:

Campbell's Black Bean Soup: *for Ellen Gallagher.* The quote *a nigger's loft* taken from *The Andy Warhol Diaries,* ed. Pat Hackett.
Poison Oasis: To be read *al dente,* slowly.
Brothers Sausage: During one of his many attempts to run away from home, Basquiat went to a state park. He soon returned.

Jack Johnson: In the voice of the first black heavyweight champion of the world, tried for "white slavery" under the Mann Act. For further reference, we suggest *Bad Nigger!,* his autobiography *Jack Johnson Is a Dandy, Jack Johnson and His Times,* and Arthur Ashe's *Hard Road to Glory.* Also "The Black Hamlet" from *Sports Illustrated,* 1959. Miles Davis recorded the score (and wrote liner notes) to the eponymous 1969 documentary, narrated by Brock Peters.

Onion Gum: To be read up tempo, *al forte.*

Charlie Chan on Horn: *for John Yau.* Since recording this single, we have learnt that CHAN appears in many a painting; Chan was also the name of Charlie Parker's wife.

Godchild Miles Davis: A bonus track that should be considered part of the eventual "box set."

Riddle Me This Batman: *for the late Jerry Badanes,* joke teller and inspiration, who passed away suddenly during the composition of this canto. The Bat represents both a sign of life and of death: Batman always in peril, about to die cliffhanger style; yet always saved, vampiric, nocturnal, death-defying.

Eroica: Latin for "heroic," "Eroica" also is the name of Beethoven's Third Symphony, originally for Napoleon Bonaparte, later for "the memory of a great man." In his research, Kevin Young realized that the definitions listed in the painting most likely came from Clarence Major's groundbreaking *Dictionary of Afro-American Slang,* from 1969.

Shrine Outside Basquiat's Studio: If you look closely, you can still see the graffito *Je t'aime Jean-Michel* written on his Great Jones Street doorbell.

Retrospective: To be read *misterioso.*

CHAMBER MUSIC (1999–2004)

Duet was first read at the wedding of Sarah & Jeff.

Hurricane Song was originally published in Poem-a-Day by the Academy of American Poets.

Election Day, Saeta, and **Chamber Music** first appeared in the *Virginia Quarterly Review.*

Strays appeared in *The Miami Rail.*

FOR THE CONFEDERATE DEAD (2007)

Guernica is *in memoriam June Jordan,* who admired it after it was published.

Throne of the Third Heaven . . . is the name of the altar made entirely of aluminum foil by self-taught artist James Hampton. Found in his garage after his death, Hampton's life work is now on view in the Smithsonian.

African Elegy is *for Philippe Wamba,* friend and author, who was killed in a car accident in Kenya on the one-year anniversary of September 11th. He was thirty-one. Philippe had just returned to the African continent, where he'd grown up and where his father and family were from, after spending a number of years in the United States of his mother's birth. This dual African and American heritage was the subject of his first book *Kinship;* he was conducting research for his second book, on contemporary Africa, when he died. "African Elegy" is an account of learning of his death, attending his funeral in his home of Tanzania, and after. The poems take their titles in part from the Bob Marley songs and reggae Philippe loved. Besides being dedicated to the memory of Philippe, the poem and this book are also for the Wamba family, his fiancée, and his many friends, who all miss him terribly.

HOMAGE TO PHILLIS WHEATLEY (1998–2011)

Excluding the newspaper notices, most all of these "Homage" poems take their titles from works by Phillis Wheatley. Much of this sequence first appeared in *The Kenyon Review.*

Before Wheatley could get her first and only book, *Poems on Various Subjects, Religious and Moral* (1773), published in London—few in the colonies would subscribe to a book by the "Negro Servant to Mr. Wheatley"—she required a document proving she was the author, signed by prominent men of Massachusetts, including John Hancock and her master, John Wheatley.

On Imagination: In the ending of this poem by Wheatley, we might see some suggestion of a middle passage, taking her from a land, here allegorized as Imagination, where "in one view we grasp the mighty whole, Or with new worlds amaze th' *unbounded* soul" (emphasis added).

> But I reluctant leave the pleasing views,
> Which Fancy *dresses to delight the* Muse;
> Winter *austere forbids me to aspire,*
> *And northern tempests damp the rising fire;*
> *They chill the tides of* Fancy's *flowing sea,*
> *Cease then, my song, cease the unequal lay.*

An Hymn to the Morning:

> *Ye shady groves, your verdant gloom display*
> *To shield your poet from the burning day:*
> Calliope *awake the sacred lyre,*
> *While thy fair sisters fan the pleasing fire:*

On the Affray in King-Street: This Wheatley poem on the Boston Massacre was advertised for a 1772 edition never realized, and that is now lost to us.

To Mr. & Mrs. ———, on the Death of Their Infant Son: Title taken from what is thought to be Wheatley's final poem, written in the last months of her life, after losing two children herself.

How would your prayers, your ardent wishes, rise,
Safe to repose him in his native skies.

Elegy on Leaving ————: The most recent poem added to the Wheatley canon, attributed to her more than two hundred years after her death.

But, ah! those pleasing hours are ever flown;
Ye scenes of transport from my thoughts retire;
Those rural joys no more the day shall crown,
No more my hand shall wake the warbling lyre.

A Farewel [sic] to America: For her health and to help promote and ensure publication of her book, Wheatley journeyed to London with a son of the Wheatley family. There she was entertained by (and entertained, to be sure) members of British high society. However, the illness of her mistress, Susannah Wheatley, ended Wheatley's trip before she had met her benefactor, the Countess of Huntingdon, or even young King George. Susannah Wheatley would die in the spring of 1774. Phillis Wheatley would follow ten years later, dying alone, impoverished, in a Boston rooming house.

For thee, Britannia, *I resign*
New-England's *smiling fields;*
To view again her charms divine,
What joy the prospect yields!

Perhaps Wheatley's best epitaph may be these lines from an homage written by her contemporary, the fellow black poet and former slave Jupiter Hammond:

While thousands muse with earthly toys;
And range beyond the street,
Dear Phillis, seek for heaven's joys,
Where we do hope to meet.

ARDENCY (2011)

For this chronicle, I relied on several historical sources, crucially John Wesley Blassingame's *Slave Testimony,* which contains the Mendi's actual letters. Two other historically reliable texts were Mary Cable's *Black Odyssey* and the fine account provided by Muriel Rukeyser in her biography of Willard Gibbs—the very one that influenced Robert Hayden's class poem "Middle Passage." John Warner Barber's fascinating original 1840 account, *A History of the Amistad Captives,* provided the illustrations included here. William Owens's fictional *Slave Mutiny* (renamed *Black Mutiny* in the 1960s) provided useful texture and occasional background along the way.

John Quincy Adams (1767–1848), Harvard man, was the only U.S. President (1825–1829) to serve in Congress (1831–1848) *after* his term in the White House. In 1841 he argued successfully before the Supreme Court to free the *Amistad* rebels rather than return them to the slave traders who bought them or give them to the navy who commandeered the mutinied ship. ("Correspondance")

Antonio, Cabin Boy (as he is often called here), was spared by the Africans during the rebellion in order to translate between the Mendi and the Spaniards who bought them. Though he was often an unreliable translator and seemed to align himself with the Spaniards, he disappeared sometime during the trial rather than remain with them in slavery. ("Exodus," "Maroon")

Captain Ferrer helmed the *Amistad* through the storms that delayed it on what should have been a brief trip from Havana to Puerto Principe. He was killed with the cook in the uprising while some of the crew escaped over the side—reportedly to reach land and tell of their ordeal. ("Buzzard," "Westville")

Celestino, the Cook on the *Amistad,* was suspected of being the son of Captain Ferrer as well as his manservant. He reportedly mimed through hand gestures that the Mendi were to be killed and eaten after leaving Cuba, which may have precipitated the mutiny by the Africans as much as the worsening conditions did. ("Friendship")

Cinque (1814–1879) was a rice planter with a wife and three children before his capture and enslavement. Roughly twenty-seven years old, he led the revolt on the *Amistad,* using a nail to free himself and others on the slave ship. Upon returning to Africa in 1842, Cinque left the mission station established by the *Amistad* Committee to search for his family. Though unsuccessful, he returned to his people's customs, apparently becoming a chief among them. Disheartened missionaries heard and passed along unfounded rumors that Cinque had reverted to "paganism" and slave trading—or returned to the mission for a deathbed conversion. ("Advent," "Witness")

The Committee to free the Mendi was organized by well-intentioned abolitionists who not only sought to free the Africans but to proselytize them to Christianity. This organization, still in existence under another name, also began the mission that returned the Amistads to Mendi. Within a short time the mission failed; the Africans abandoned it, presumably to find their families. ("Broadway")

James Covey, translator for the captured Mendi, was discovered on the docks by one of the abolitionists who searched for a native speaker by counting to ten in Mendi. As a young man, Covey himself had been captured and then saved by a British ship and returned to Freetown. At that time, the international slave trade was officially illegal (though one could still be born into chattel slavery, a loophole particular to the Americas); of course, unofficially the trade was sanctioned if not by law then by action and inaction. Covey speaks not as a prisoner but to and for the Mendi. ("Buzzard")

Fu-li, a fellow Mendi, was apparently branded by Captain Ferrer ("Exodus") and later converted to Christianity, even changing his name. ("Gentleman")

Kale was the youngest of the *Amistad* captives, and one of the first to learn English. Often he was asked to spell words and religious phrases to prove both the Mendi's devotion and intelligence. ("Broadway," "Westville")

Kin-na was an unmarried young man when kidnapped on the War Road. ("New Haven")

The Spaniards Montes and Ruiz bought the Amistads, mostly Mendi, from a trader in Cuba. Because even in Cuba newly captured African slaves (*bozales*) were illegal, the men forged papers, giving the Mendi Christian and Spanish names in order to pretend they were *ladinos* born in Cuba.

Steele was one of the white missionaries sent to Sierra Leone with the Amistads in order to establish a mission. ("Soundings," "Gentleman")

Lewis Tappan was a white abolitionist who championed the Amistads' cause. He is an important American figure, discussed at length by poet Muriel Rukeyser in her biography of Willard Gibbs. The Mendi wrote him seeking aid in their release. ("Correspondance")

Tucker was a local leader in Sierra Leone near the original mission. Appeasing him was customary, but morally fraught for some of the missionaries. ("Gentleman")

RAPTURE (2009–2013)

Wedding Song was first read at the wedding of Aaron & Niesha Foster.

Anthem was commissioned by NPR as part of their News Poets program, and written and read on *All Things Considered* on March 30, 2012.

Whole Hog is in memoriam Jake Adam York and first appeared in *Gravy*.

A Short Blessing for a Long Marriage was first read at the wedding of Julie Barer & Colson Whitehead.

There Is a Light That Never Goes Out is the title of a song by the Smiths and first appeared in *Virginia Quarterly Review*.

Rapture first appeared in *The New Yorker*.

A NOTE ABOUT THE AUTHOR

Kevin Young is the author of ten books of poetry, including *Book of Hours,* winner of the Lenore Marshall Poetry Prize from the Academy of American Poets and a finalist for the Kingsley Tufts Award; *Ardency: A Chronicle of the* Amistad *Rebels,* winner of a 2012 American Book Award; and *Jelly Roll: A Blues,* a finalist for the National Book Award. He is also the editor of eight other collections, most recently *The Hungry Ear: Poems of Food & Drink.*

Young's book *The Grey Album: On the Blackness of Blackness* won the Graywolf Nonfiction Prize, was a *New York Times* Notable Book and a finalist for the National Book Critics Circle Award for criticism, and won the PEN Open Book Award. He is currently the Charles Howard Candler Professor of Creative Writing and English and curator of both Literary Collections and the Raymond Danowski Poetry Library at Emory University.

A NOTE ON THE TYPE

The text of this book was composed in Apollo, the first typeface ever originated specifically for film composition. Designed by Adrian Frutiger and issued by the Monotype Corporation of London in 1964, Apollo is not only a versatile typeface suitable for many uses but also pleasant to read in all of its sizes.

Composed by North Market Street Graphics,
Lancaster, Pennsylvania

Printed and bound by Berryville Graphics, Berryville, Virginia

Designed by Maggie Hinders

ML   3-16